BLOODHOUND IN BLUE

JJ and Officer Serio

BLOODHOUND
IN BLUE

THE TRUE TALES OF POLICE DOG JJ
AND HIS TWO-LEGGED PARTNER

ADAM DAVID RUSS

For David —
Thanks for the
skilled feedback and traveling
this writer's journey
with me.
With deep
admiration and
appreciation,

LP

LYONS PRESS
Guilford, Connecticut
An imprint of Globe Pequot Press

Lyons Press is an imprint of Globe Pequot Press.

Text design: Maggie Peterson
Layout: Melissa Evarts
Project editors: Ellen Urban and Lauren Brancato

Frontispiece photo courtesy of Salt Lake City Police Department

Library of Congress Cataloging-in-Publication Data

Russ, Adam David.
  Bloodhound in blue : the true tales of police dog JJ and his two-legged partner
/ Adam David Russ.
      pages cm
  Includes bibliographical references and index.
  ISBN 978-0-7627-8538-4
  1. Police dogs. I. Title.
  HV8025.R8697 2013
  363.28—dc23

                                                                    2013014994

Printed in the United States of America

10 9 8 7 6 5 4 3 2 1

For Kadee,

and with love to Atticus

And though the villain 'scape a while, he feels
Slow vengeance, like a bloodhound, at his heels.

—Jonathan Swift

I've already had medical attention.
A dog licked me when I was on the ground.

—Neil Simon

CONTENTS

AUTHOR'S NOTE

This book is a work of nonfiction. The stories are real and backed by police case records, news reports, and firsthand accounts of many of those involved. The dialogue in the book comes from individuals speaking, draws upon their best memory, or was quoted in news sources and reports. The name of any crime victim not already known to the public has been changed. All other names are real.

The Bloodhound Breed Standards appearing at the start of each chapter are attributed to Dr. Sidney Turner and Mr. Edwin Brough in *Points and Characteristics of the Bloodhound or Sleuth-hound*. Published in 1894, the descriptions are still used today in evaluating bloodhounds by both the Kennel Club of the United Kingdom and the American Kennel Club.

INTRODUCTION
PEDIGREE

Like Mark Twain, Jessie Jr. was born in a small town in rural Missouri. Other than a prominent nose and perhaps a shared affinity for porterhouse steak, the similarities end there. His mother and father were nothing if not prolific and gave him nine siblings to fight and play with when he was first learning the ways of the world. Although they came so close together no one remembers his exact place in the birth order, it was clear early on that Jessie Jr. was different from the rest.

Mozart is said to have played the clavier flawlessly by age four and began composing music at the age of five. John von Neumann, the renowned mathematician and principal contributor to the Manhattan Project's development of the atomic bomb, was deemed a mental calculator at age six who liked to tell jokes in Ancient Greek. While rare by definition, prodigies are most common in the arts and sciences. In this Jessie Jr. set himself further apart. His field of expertise was law enforcement. He caught his first criminal—an intoxicated hit-and-run suspect—at age two. By his sixth birthday he had successfully tracked down missing children, drug dealers, burglars, thieves, kidnappers, armed robbers, batterers, rapists, child molesters, and murderers, including Utah's most wanted criminal—all on his way to becoming one of the top police dogs in the country.

Known by family and friends as JJ, by law enforcement personnel throughout the West as Officer Serio's canine partner, and by captured criminals as "that damned dog," Jessie Jr., an exceptionally talented bloodhound, loved his job. His distinctive voice, a deep, reverberating bay sounding like a sea lion that had swallowed a foghorn, let everyone in earshot know that JJ had found the track and was on his way.

More than a prodigy, JJ was a pioneer. Although a small minority of police departments, primarily in the South and East, have used bloodhounds, the breed rarely had been deployed as police dogs in the West and never in Utah. The prevailing opinion held by Utah's police K9 handlers, who work with the fearsomely efficient German and Belgian shepherds, was that bloodhounds were "floppy-eared dogs that don't bite." Not biting, it was believed, rendered them useless for police work. To be fair, at least some of the blame for the officers' negative opinion of a bloodhound's capabilities can, as with many of today's misconceptions and head-scratching platitudes, fall on country music.

George Jones started the lie. Kenny Rogers picked it up a few years later, and then, in a move that some say launched his career, Blake Shelton—now known for such hits as "I Drink," "The More I Drink," and "Kiss My Country Ass"—sang the lie all the way up to number fourteen on Billboard's chart of Hot Country Songs. The song containing the lie in question is "Ol'

Red." It tells the tale of a hound dog owned by the warden at a prison farm in Georgia that tracks down anyone foolish enough to try to escape.

Granted the song is a fiction created by songwriters Bo Bohan, Don Goodman, and Mark Sherrill, yet it contains elements that our culture has assimilated as truth. It doesn't help that many bloodhound handlers, with aspirations of helping the police, make the same mythical claims of their dogs' smelling multiple-day-old trails. Even our pals across the pond believe the fantasy. *The Times* of London, reporting on two bloodhounds joining a UK police force—the first such police dogs in the kingdom in over sixty years—stated that the dogs "will be able to pick up a trail that is several days old and follow it for up to 24 hours."

Unsolved crimes, particularly sensational ones involving children, bring out of the woodwork armchair criminal profilers, psychics of every hue, and concerned citizens calling in false leads on creepy neighbors. Into the fray come bloodhound handlers claiming that their dogs could find Jimmy Hoffa if you just let them sniff the old teamster's shoe.

Time and again police officers have seen bold claims of a bloodhound's skills come to nothing. Under such intense public scrutiny, it's understandable that they refuse to integrate the overhyped floppy-eared dogs into their law enforcement teams. For JJ resistance took the form of doubt, ridicule, distrust, and jealousy. When he finally won over naysayers years later, JJ and his handler ran into something much worse: the crushing despair of failure amid high hopes.

As with many child stars, unrealistic expectations eventually derail a rapid rise to lasting glory. However, unlike a young star whose talent fails to hold, the consequences of JJ's coming up short had higher stakes, notably in the lost track of Brian David Mitchell, the man who abducted fourteen-year-old Elizabeth Smart from her Salt Lake City home, raped her, and held her captive for nine months. After she was found and reunited with her family, the FBI and SLCPD investigators interviewed Elizabeth about the day of the kidnapping. While she was being taken on foot to a remote camp in the mountains, Elizabeth says she heard a dog baying in the woods behind her. JJ was pulled off the track for several reasons, all of them rationally sound but tragically wrong.

Nevertheless, his proven abilities changed the landscape of how the region's police departments deploy their resources to capture bad guys. JJ's efforts in almost nine years of service to the greater Salt Lake City community resulted in the apprehension of nearly three hundred criminal suspects. More than just brute force and technology, good police work also contains elements of art and serendipity that can come only by way of talented humans and, when the conditions are right, through well-trained tracking dogs.*

While JJ, Utah's first police bloodhound, had an extraordinary record that may be hard to replicate, we can see his greatest success in the ripple effects. At least eight police departments—with a total of sixteen working bloodhounds to date—directly attribute the upgrade of their K9 programs to JJ and his partner, Officer Michael Serio. This is their story, fleas and all.

---

* See *Notes and Sources* for "tracking" vs. "trailing."

PART ONE

ROOKIES AND PUPPIES

You cannot run with the hare and hunt with the hounds.

—Proverb

GENERAL CHARACTER

The Bloodhound possesses, in a most marked degree, every point and characteristic of those dogs which hunt together by scent. He is very powerful, and stands over more ground than is usual with hounds of other breeds.

November 2003

"All units, be advised: Salt Lake County Sheriff's Office is in pursuit of a homicide suspect in the neighborhood of 1700 South 400 East. They are requesting that City officers respond to the area to assist."

The dispatch came across all channels shortly before 1:00 a.m. Preceded by three long beeps, signaling an event in progress, it was sure to raise the pulse of any officer within a fifteen-minute radius of the location. Given Salt Lake City's relatively small size, with a population of just under 190,000 and an urban layout on a grid plan, this meant most everyone working the graveyard shift that night. The city's wide streets, the stuff of legend, date back to its origins in the mid-1800s. Brigham Young, the "Mormon Moses" who led his people on a westward exodus to settle finally on the banks of the Great Salt Lake—the closest thing to the Dead Sea anywhere else on earth—wanted streets wide enough that a wagon team could turn around without "resorting to profanity."

Officer Mike Serio, driving a half-ton Chevy Silverado truck with a turning radius not much better than a wagon team, heard the dispatch and headed toward the reported location. Not known for using expletives lightly, Serio resorted to profanity several times before the night ended. His police truck came specially equipped for K9 teams, with an eject button on the dash that released a cage door on the back of the truck. The patrol dog could "deploy dynamically" and catch a fleeing suspect on the run. JJ never rode in the back of the truck, though, and the idea of a bloodhound deploying dynamically was better to ponder than actually do. If he wasn't sitting on the passenger seat getting double takes from other motorists and pedestrians, JJ was likely curled up on the rear bench seat, fast asleep. It caused no end of ribbing for Serio from his fellow officers when he showed up at a crime scene.

Lights blazing everywhere from a multitude of police, fire, and medical vehicles; radios squawking orders and updates; neighbors congregating on nearby lawns and peering from doorways, the scenes all had a well-practiced chaos with an energy all their own. Into the commotion Serio pulled up in his truck, emblazoned with "K9 Squad" in bright, bold letters on all sides. As often happened, he'd have to wake up his partner, who would gingerly emerge from the truck, yawn, and stretch in a series of ancient dog poses that have inspired countless yoga routines from Bangkok to Berkeley.

Fortunately, on this night JJ was already awake and, if not yet eager, at least ready for action. Serio had taken JJ out to investigate a separate sighting of a possible suspect in a nearby neighborhood shortly after he learned that county officers had lost the vehicle they were pursuing. Ten minutes later Dispatch reported the homicide suspect's vehicle found, but neither driver nor passenger were anywhere in sight. Serio didn't go directly to the scene because he had heard that county K9 officers had their dogs out, and he wouldn't tread on their turf unless they asked. He continued to work where he was, but JJ had no interest in the possible sighting. He was just out for a walk.

"Hey, Mike," called Serio's boss, Sergeant Jon Richey, over the radio, "I'm down at the scene. Don't worry about that sighting. Let's get you down here to the car where we know these bad guys were."

Sergeant Richey, head of the Salt Lake City K9 Squad, had arrived at the scene of the abandoned vehicle and watched as two county K9 officers with their German shepherds attempted to pick up a track. Seeing that they weren't having any luck, he approached them.

"The car has been here ten, maybe fifteen, minutes," Richey said. "They're not going to be hiding in the next yard. If you want to get a good bead on these guys, put your dogs away, and wait for the bloodhound and Officer Serio to show up."

Trained to apprehend uncooperative suspects, German shepherds also sniff out narcotics, firearms, explosives, cadavers, and living humans. They excel at this last skill within a contained area such as a building or a neighborhood block. Some have tracked suspects beyond a contained block, but it's not their specialty. But every handler believes that his dog is best. It's a belief necessary for success, as if the dog requires the unwavering confidence to do its job, but that doesn't always leave room for cooperation with other dog handlers.

Coming from anyone else, the county K9 officers might have responded to someone telling them to put up their dogs with the tight-wagon-turn equivalent of "Go fly a kite," but they complied. Sergeant Richey had been training police dogs longer than anyone else in the Salt Lake Valley. He started many of the active dog programs. He had earned the respect they showed him. Although renowned as an expert with shepherds, his experience with bloodhounds consisted only of what he had seen with Serio and JJ. Others in the police K9 community resisted or doubted bloodhounds, but Richey's philosophy about using four-legged animals to capture two-legged criminals was simple: "Whatever works. I don't care if it's a fucking pig."

"Come on, JJ, this is a big one," Serio said nervously to his partner on the drive over. "We've got to do good on this one." Richey had put his neck out for them. Serio was relatively new to the K9 unit, and Richey as department head was newer still.

Standing six-foot-two and weighing 210 pounds only if he happened to be wearing nine-inch platforms while carrying a fifty-pound bag of dog food over his shoulder, Serio was one of the shortest police officers on the force. JJ, on the other hand, was taller, longer, and a good ten pounds heavier than his fellow police dogs—though still on the lean side for bloodhounds. He combined regal and goofy in the same expression, and even the reticent couldn't help but smile at his approach. Bystanders' smiles often disappeared, however, when JJ's affable greeting left thick, sticky strands of translucent drool everywhere.

The county K9 officers watched Serio and JJ arrive, but they stood to the side. Richey gave Serio a determined look, his briefing all business. "That's the suspect vehicle. It's been here for about fifteen minutes. We have no idea which direction they went. It's all yours."

Parked on the street with asphalt on one side and a concrete sidewalk on the other, the car wasn't in the easiest spot to start a track. An ideal start is when a suspect gets out of a car and runs across a big grassy field, but that's a rare luxury in the city. Concrete and pavement don't hold odor as well as vegetation, but JJ had been well trained in this environment, so he wasn't on unfamiliar ground.

Serio began the short routine. He sat JJ down and double-checked his harness, leather with a padded chest plate and a D-ring on the center of his back where the leash is hooked. The idea is to minimize any directional influence on the dog when tracking. Once satisfied, Serio looked at JJ and asked, "Do you want to go to *work?*" JJ immediately bellowed, perhaps foreign at first hearing but instantly recognizable. Serio stuck JJ's nose inside the car on the driver's side and let him get a good whiff.

It's surprising how little time a trailing dog spends at the intro-duction of a scent. The movies depict this scene with a bit of exag-geration: A sequence of carefully choreographed camera angles shows the dog inhaling like a wine connoisseur while dramatic notes in the musical score drive the point home—the dog has picked up a scent. Once Serio directs JJ's nose toward the driver's seat and tells him to get to work, he's on it for less than a second before whipping his head around to look for a track leaving the car. Using a fifteen-foot lead, Serio, not unlike a fly fisherman, casts JJ in different directions emanating from the car.

JJ seemed to pick up something heading east behind a nearby house. Sergeant Richey, following ten to twenty feet behind so as not to get in the way, repeatedly asked, "Is this it? Is this it? You got it?"

"Hang on," Serio responded each time. "I don't know yet."

JJ followed the track across the street, turned the corner—and then stopped. It was if he was saying, "Nope, that's not it." Serio took him back to the car and checked westbound through the front yard of another house. No luck there, either. In hindsight Serio suspects that JJ was following the trails of the different offi-cers and canines that initially searched the area. Even though JJ had been presented the inside of the suspect's car as the scent to follow, it's natural for the dog to inventory all the smells and where they lead until, in theory, he either matches the scent inside the car or picks up the track going farthest away from the scene.

While JJ showed some interest in the first few tracks, he hadn't signaled to Serio yet that he'd found what he wanted. On the next cast JJ sniffed a track slowly and methodically north-bound across a paved driveway that led to a tall wooden fence between two houses. When he got to the fence, his tail started wagging; he jumped up and down a bit; and he put his front paws on the fence. Serio waited a minute, wanting to be sure. Sensing his master's hesitation, JJ let out a really big bay.

That's what Serio had been hoping for. He could finally answer Sergeant Richey's repeated question. "I'm pretty sure they went over this fence."

Serio and JJ could navigate most fences they encountered by themselves, but this one, over six feet high, required some able-bodied assistance. Shepherds can make an assisted jump like this gracefully, but with ninety pounds of gangly bloodhound, it's not pretty. Serio climbed the fence and waited on the other side. JJ put his paws up on the fence as high as he dared, about two feet shy of the top. Richey scooped up JJ's hind legs and pushed his butt up and over. Serio caught him in a barely controlled collapse.

Once over the fence, his legs safely beneath him, JJ hooked into the track with gusto, baying left and right. Serio immediately got on his radio, a device strapped to his chest that required just the push of a button. "I've got a hot track headed north from the suspect vehicle to the next street."

In their patrol cars county and city officers began scouting the area a few blocks ahead of JJ's location in the hope of either getting a visual on the suspects or, using their overhead lights as advertisement, scaring them to ground so that the canines could do what they do best. The longer a suspect stays on the move, the higher the chances of losing the track.

Officer Barry Larsen, another Salt Lake City K9 officer, had been waiting for Serio's call back at the scene with Aldo, his five-year-old German shepherd. The city's street patrol dogs would be used instead of the county's because they were already familiar with working with a bloodhound. Larsen and Aldo caught up to the track in progress quickly, running anywhere from five to forty-five feet behind Serio and JJ as circumstances warranted.

A patrol dog follows closely behind for three primary reasons. Foremost is protection. There's nothing stealthy about a baying bloodhound yanking his handler behind him. While actively tracking, both are exposed and, at least temporarily, defenseless against the potentially armed individuals they are chasing. The patrol dog team allows them to focus all their energies on finding and following the trail. Second is speed. If the suspect flushes, the patrol dog can catch him. Third is another nose. Sometimes the bloodhound focuses so much on the scent of one suspect that he might miss another suspect who splits off and hides in the bushes. JJ could blow right by someone hiding while following the trail of another person. If this happens, the patrol dog can pick up the scent of the guy in the bushes and lead to him. This is what happened that night— or so they thought.

After navigating the fence and heading northbound to the next block, JJ followed a track that cut to the left along the sidewalk. He was baying and pulling hard, so Serio knew they were following a strong track in that direction.

"Hey," Larsen called out behind them, "I've got something here."

Aldo picked up an air scent that led off the track that JJ had been following. Larsen knew his dog well, and Aldo, barking up a storm, was clearly alerting to something or someone beneath a camper trailer parked off the street in a large side yard. Serio stopped for a few seconds to look back, but JJ continued westbound, so they kept going, knowing that they could still be tracking the other suspect.

Richey peeled off with Larsen and Aldo to provide assistance. They saw a man lying beneath the camper and lit him up with flashlights.

"Salt Lake City Police Department!" Larsen called out. "Show me your hands, show me your hands!"

No hands.

Larsen let his dog go, and before you could say, "That's gonna hurt," Aldo dashed under the camper and attached himself by the jaws to the man's arm. Knowing the suspects were reported as armed and dangerous, Larsen and Aldo did what they were supposed to do when the man didn't comply with a direct challenge. Unfortunately for everyone involved—especially the man under the trailer—he wasn't one of the suspects. It took the officers a while to sort out that the man whom Aldo had bitten was homeless and happened to pick the underside of a camper as the best place to sleep for the night. By that time Serio and JJ were gone, alone and unprotected.

JJ continued tracking west for another two blocks before doing a buttonhook to the left and dragging Serio into a narrow alley between two houses. Concerned about not having backup and heading into a dark yard at 1:30 in the morning on a track that probably led to at least one of the reportedly armed suspects, Serio got on the radio. "Hey, guys, I'm still on this track. Get me some help here."

Behind the houses JJ's head popped up, and he started doing the "Stevie Wonder," the term that K9 handlers use when a scenting dog gets caught up in a cloud of a human's air scent. JJ's head was waving back and forth while he pranced left and right, sniffing the air. Serio knew that the suspect was close, that he had probably gone to ground and was hiding nearby. When an individual stays in one place, the scent coming off his body has time to build, pool in the air, and drift around, no longer leaving a linear trail. A dog has to work the edge of the scent cloud until he can isolate its origin. This is the most vulnerable time for both dog and handler because they don't know where the suspect is hiding, but he knows exactly where they are.

Serio drew his gun and frantically looked around, trying to spot the guy while still attempting to work JJ along the scent trail. Because it was too dark to see much, he dropped JJ's leash and took out his flashlight, aiming it high and low in all directions. Too many places to hide. JJ swung to the right and ran to a three-foot chain-link fence enclosing the adjacent backyard. Baying to beat the band, JJ wanted over that fence. Serio lit up the area and noticed a boat on an unattached trailer. He also noticed someone underneath one of the wheel wells of the trailer.

"Salt Lake City Police!" Serio yelled, aiming his gun at the man. "Let me see your hands. Get your fucking hands in the air right now!"

Officer Randy Hunnewell arrived to provide much-needed backup. Then Larsen and Aldo came full speed into the backyard. JJ was baying; Aldo was barking; Serio, Hunnewell, and Larsen were issuing challenges and yelling at the guy to comply. Both Serio and Hunnewell had drawn their weapons on the suspect. With two hands Larsen was holding onto Aldo, still juiced from his previous bite and itching for another. Pumped with adrenaline, sensing the frenzied commotion from all the yelling, and frustrated at not being released, Aldo reached up between Serio's legs and bit him on the inner thigh.

Serio was thankful that the police academy had trained him always to keep his trigger finger on the side of the gun until he had made a conscious decision to shoot. He also was thankful that Aldo didn't give him a full bite, just "a slight, small puncture with some scraping." But it still hurt like hell.

Outnumbered by at least twelve legs, the homicide suspect beneath the boat finally complied with the officers' requests.

They took him into custody without further incident. His partner was caught shortly after by a patrol officer driving a few blocks ahead of Serio's location.

Drug possessions, stolen vehicles, burglaries, armed robberies, multiple counts of aggravated assault with a deadly weapon, and more—the arrested suspects were career criminals with a combined total of more than 20 arrests and 110 charges over the previous two decades. Odds are likely that they would have been caught somewhere down the line, after committing some other crime, but they would have escaped that night if not for a bloodhound's unique gifts and his handler's long bout to prove their worth.

TEMPERAMENT

In temperament he is extremely affectionate, neither quarrelsome with companions nor with other dogs. His nature is somewhat shy, and equally sensitive to kindness or correction by his master.

March 1997

We enter the world led by the nose. Even before birth, a baby's sense of smell is the means by which the amniotic surroundings are most acutely experienced, and once out of the womb, it is smell that allows an infant to distinguish his mother from an entire squadron of women passing him around. The nose's reign is short-lived, however, as sight, sound, and touch quickly surpass it in the sensory rankings. Not wanting to be left alone at the bottom, however, smell so thoroughly intertwines itself with taste that it claims responsibility for up to 80 percent of the flavors we can discern.

As with any ability, the power of the nose varies from person to person, but even a champion Cyrano de Bergerac model pales in comparison to most noses in the animal kingdom. The disparity is markedly noted when considering the capacity of canines. Your average Joe Terrier can smell a scent well over a hundred times as keenly as a human, and top dog of them all, the bloodhound, has a nose a *thousand* times more sensitive than yours or mine. With our paltry sniffers it may be hard to conceive just what "a thousand times better" means, so a visual analogy may help. If a five-foot-five police officer represented the human nose, the nose of a bloodhound would tower more than a mile tall. A dog's nose is a miraculous thing.

Sired by Jed's Ole Duke and mothered by Ellie Mae's Duchess, JJ descended from royalty in name only. Born in the rural flatlands of Missouri, he and his nine siblings soon went off to the big city surrounded by Utah's Wasatch Mountains. First, JJ's five sisters found homes with other families. A man who wanted a bloodhound for hunting mountain lions snapped up his brother, the biggest of the litter, but that didn't worry JJ. He was happy to stay with his remaining three brothers. But then JJ was picked next. Only he had a big white spot of fur on his chest, and he had beautiful eyes rimmed with markings that looked like eyeliner flawlessly applied. But it was his nose that did it. He kept wandering off from the rest of the pups, smelling all the good smells and finding where they led. Serio and his girlfriend, Lisa, intrigued, took note. The next thing JJ knew, he was in their car, being taken away. He let out a bay that, unbeknownst to all, soon became his signature and howled the entire trip home.

Eight weeks old, ten pounds of wrinkled skin and soft fur, JJ had a face that any mother could love—but only a select few would want in their home. In the category of best pets recommended for families, bloodhounds don't make the list. Although good-natured and gentle to a fault—tolerating all manner of abuse from children—bloodhounds are large and powerful dogs that are slow to mature, slow to obey, and quick to chew and swallow things that make emergency trips to the veterinarian a common excursion.

Then there's the drool.

Even the most ardent dog lovers have a hard time dealing with the never-ending stream of slobber that coats everything within reach and frequently appears in higher places, as thick globules shoot from the chops at the shake of the head.

Serio, however, didn't know all this at the time—or at least not the full extent of what he was in for. Like a conscientious parent, Serio had read all he could find on proper bloodhound care and nutrition; he meticulously chose doctors and potential caregivers; and he devoted significant resources and energy to puppy-proofing his house to keep young JJ out of harm's way. He failed, however, as many criminals also failed to do in the years to come, to fully appreciate JJ's tenacity—his innate drive to seek and find.

JJ was the only puppy in the litter that had a big white spot of fur on his chest. He also had beautiful black-rimmed eyes, but it was his nose that did it. *Photograph courtesy of Mike and Lisa Serio*

In the first few weeks after they got him, Serio and Lisa tried to arrange their schedules so that at least one of them was with JJ all the time, but that wasn't always possible. They positioned JJ's sleeping crate so that he could exit through the doggy door directly into a long fenced-in kennel in the backyard. It was a perfect setup . . . for about a week. Serio and Lisa came home one day to find their house a little messier than usual. The pantry door in the kitchen was wide open, and the place had a sense of clumsy disorder. It didn't require a detective to determine that JJ had gotten out of his crate, but he wasn't any longer inside the house. Serio found his puppy in the backyard.

Happy to see him and blithely untouched by guilt, JJ rushed over with his usual full-body wag. But the greeting seemed to require additional effort. His stomach was huge! Serio ran his hand along JJ's side and belly and could feel small, hard bumps. There wasn't a cushy spot in his solid-as-a-rock stomach. Serio first thought that JJ had somehow swallowed river rocks from the yard. Then he found the remnants of a twenty-five-pound bag of Hill's Prescription Diet t/d Canine Bites. Specifically designed, the dense chicken-nugget-sized dog treats reduce tartar buildup and bad breath and scrub away plaque.

JJ's breath smelled great, but Serio worried about bloat. Bloodhounds are particularly susceptible to the dangerous condition technically known as gastric dilatation-volvulus. Often triggered by wolfing down food or overeating, something goes wrong during digestion. Gases build in the stomach so fast that the stomach itself stretches dangerously, cutting off blood circulation. The stomach can also twist and turn, trapping the gas inside. Untreated, bloat can quickly lead to cardiac arrest and death.

Serio rushed JJ to the Willow Creek Veterinary Center. The X-ray of JJ's stomach resembled what an X-ray of an unopened

Day 1—Serio brings JJ home as an 8-week-old puppy.
Photograph courtesy of Mike and Lisa Serio

twenty-five-pound bag of dog treats must look like. At least 90 percent of the treats still in JJ's stomach were fully intact. The puppy had swallowed them whole. The vet said that bloat wasn't common in puppies and recommended that Serio wait and see. Serio waited and saw. JJ pooped pile after pile of nuggets, mostly undigested, for the next two days.

He didn't need it that time, but Serio learned early with JJ to carry hydrogen peroxide with him wherever they went. Not to be used lightly—only with 3 percent peroxide and only upon veterinarian recommendation—it can literally be a lifesaver: The dog truly empties his entire stomach. Serio remembers all seven times with JJ, often in Technicolor detail.

But the puppy soon discovered a favorite activity. He jumped on top of Lisa, distracted her with slobbery kisses, grabbed her hair scrunchy, and ran. Fast and nimble though he was, he eventually got caught and had to give up his prize. Combining both crafty intelligence and colossal stupidity, JJ quickly learned that the only way to keep his treasure was to swallow it. JJ applied this logic to pantyhose, wild mushrooms, an empty beer can used to capture grease drippings from the grill, telephone wires, a coaxial cable for the TV, the wire harness for an air conditioning unit, and a flytrap with thousands of dead flies, along with the rancid hamburger meat used to attract them. It wasn't pretty.

• • •

The loyal and lovable Labrador retriever is America's top dog in terms of sheer numbers and—hard to argue—fame. The German shepherd bounds close on the Labrador's haunches in both categories. Terriers, beagles, bulldogs, boxers, dachshunds, and poodles, breeds both ubiquitous and well known, also top the list. Bloodhounds, however, are that goofy kid in high school whom everybody knows but who rarely gets invited to parties. The American Kennel Club keeps tabs on who's hot and who's not, maintaining a registry of 167 dog breeds officially recognized as purebred. The bloodhound ranks forty-third. Not too shabby, you might think . . . until you realize that numbers 44 through 167 are largely populated by such breeds as Spinoni Italiani, vendéens, pulik, and Beaucerons—names that look like exotic dishes on the menu at that snazzy new restaurant downtown. *More* popular than the bloodhound, we find vizslas, Leonbergers ("I'll have that medium rare with a side of fries, please"), Havanese, and, if you can believe it, bichon frises.

The curious combination of rarity and identifiability means that bloodhounds can empathize with celebrities. They draw attention. People flocked to JJ, invariably laughed, said something about his ears, and then asked Serio a series of questions.

"Why?" was easy enough to answer but probably took the longest to explain. Serio had decided on a bloodhound because of Jessie, his college roommate's dog. Rescued from the pound, Jessie was a hound mix that Serio had helped raise from puppyhood. Serio remembers seeing Jessie looking down at him—head poked through the railings of the stairs leading to the loft in their apartment—gravity pulling her ears down low and accentuating the folds of her face and jowls. Years later, when he was looking for a dog of his own, he wanted to find one just like Jessie, but he could only guess at the percentage and particular breed of hound in her bloodline. He decided to go to the source: the bloodhound.

The origins of a particular dog breed are difficult to pin down—that is, unless you go back far enough. Given the sheer variety of dogs in the world today, from a fully grown 5-pound

Chihuahua that looks nervous just to be alive to a 250-pound English mastiff that wonders what the worry is all about, it's incredible to realize that all of them come from the same stock, the wolf. While the DNA evidence linking all dogs to the wolf is universally accepted, conjectures abound as to the different journeys they took from there.

For the bloodhound, regarded as the oldest of the hounds, we go back to Belgium at the turn of the first millennium. We revere monks for their spiritual devotion, low-maintenance wardrobes, brew-making skills, and even pea analysis, but they are less well known for their dog breeding. Bloodhounds have the Abbey of Saint-Hubert in southern Belgium to thank for their existence.

A couple of centuries after they perfected the breed, some-time around the year AD 1200, the Saint-Hubert monks began sending pairs of bloodhounds, by then called Saint-Hubert hounds, to the king of France annually—not to slobber on him, as perhaps more than one Frenchman has guessed, but as a gift. The gift wasn't always well received. King Charles IX, a young man not accustomed to keeping negative opinions to himself, snarked that, as hunting dogs, "the St. Hubert's are more suit-able for a man with gout to follow, but not for those who wish to shorten the life of the hunted animal." Nevertheless, the gifts of the hounds from Saint-Hubert continued at least until 1789, when the French Revolution saw to it that there were no longer any ungrateful French monarchs to receive them. By that time, however, the bloodhound had established its place in Britain.

While the British also used the bloodhound for hunting ani-mals—they were typically kept on a leash to find the deer or boar before other dogs went in for the kill—they are the first reported to use bloodhounds to track humans. Sleuth hounds, as bloodhounds were often called in medieval England, are said to have been used by the English to follow such high-value targets as the king of Scotland himself, Robert the Bruce, and the wily William Wallace, later made even wilier by Mel Gibson in blue face paint.

From Robert Boyle, the seventeenth-century English scientist, we get the first written account of a bloodhound's trailing abilities. Boyle described with astonishment a bloodhound demonstration in which a dog followed a hired man's scent trail for seven miles—the last of it through a heavily populated market town—directly to the man in the upper room of a house. Despite Boyle's enthusiastic account, the use of the bloodhound in England markedly diminished with the extinction of the wild boar, a decline in deer hunting, and increased rural-to-urban migration in the 1800s.

The bloodhound lineage, having successfully survived its continental decline, once again needed a new home in which to thrive. Bloodhounds caught a ride on the European immigration wave of the mid-nineteenth century and started to make a name for themselves in the New World.

Harriet Beecher Stowe's antislavery novel, *Uncle Tom's Cabin*, appeared in 1852. The second best-selling book of its century, following only the Bible, it takes credit for fueling the abolitionist cause and helping to lay the groundwork for the Civil War. Many decades later, when the age of cinema dawned, it was the most filmed story of the silent film era, with at least nine known adaptations between 1903 and 1927. The story certainly had an impact, including, for our purposes, what it did to the reputation of bloodhounds.

Stowe carries the brunt of the blame from many self-professed bloodhound historians, but in her defense she never names the breed once in her novel. She only refers to the four-legged beasts that she so thoroughly villainizes as "dogs," as in the following scene where the slave catcher, Loker, and some men are talking about Eliza, the slave who has recently fled with her infant son:

> *"I s'pose you've got good dogs," said Haley.*
>
> *"First rate," said Marks. "But what's the use? You han't got nothin' o' hers to smell on."*
>
> *"Yes, I have," said Haley triumphantly. "Here's her shawl she left on the bed in her hurry; she left her bonnet, too."*
>
> *"That ar's lucky," said Loker; "fork over."*
>
> *"Though the dogs might damage the gal, if they come on her unawares," said Haley.*
>
> *"That ar's a consideration," said Marks. "Our dogs tore a feller half to pieces, once down in Mobile, 'fore we could get 'em off."*

Whether Stowe had bloodhounds in mind when she wrote the book is anyone's guess, although later in the story the dogs have a "hoarse, savage bay" when trailing two other runaway slaves, so you could make the argument. What is certain is that those who produced stage performances and films of *Uncle Tom's Cabin* used bloodhounds to play the dogs. The widespread popularity of the story in its various forms firmly imprinted the image of viciousness upon the bloodhound name for many years to follow.

Movies such as *I Am a Fugitive from a Chain Gang* (1932) starring Paul Muni, *The Defiant Ones* (1958) with Tony Curtis and Sidney Poitier, and *Cool Hand Luke* (1967) featuring Paul Newman in an Academy Award–nominated role all depict bloodhounds as aggressive dogs chasing prison escapees fleeing for their lives. Mickey Mouse's dog, Pluto, provided a foil to the bloodthirsty reputation of the breed throughout the 1930s, '40s, and '50s, but his jowls were drawn too short and ears too thin to connect him immediately with a real bloodhound in the minds of many viewers. Duke, the Clampetts' family dog in *The Beverly Hillbillies* (1962–71), took a bite out of the bestial reputation of the bloodhound, but perhaps he took it too far, portrayed as incurably lazy.

Despite the wide-ranging portrayals of the temperament of the breed over the last century and a half, the one characteristic in common among them all is the bloodhound's unmatched sense of smell. It remains the dog of choice when hunting humans.

HEIGHT

The mean average height of adult dogs is 26 inches. Dogs usually vary from 25 inches to 27 inches; but the greater height is to be preferred, provided that character and quality are also combined.

April 1997

The female dog, called a "bitch" or "dam" by those in the breeding industry (and "female dog" by those who have a hard time disassociating the pejorative), have litters of up to fifteen pups. The puppies are small at birth—about a pound apiece for bloodhounds—and their feet are dainty. But they don't stay small for long.

Conventional wisdom holds that by as early as two months you can predict a dog's adult height by the size of its paws. Take two puppies of equal age and size, and compare their feet. The one that looks like a four-legged circus clown is going to be big.

JJ's paws, like those of most large breeds when starting out, were disproportionate to the rest of his body. Great when standing still, the extra large paws provided a solid foundation and gave the impression of firm balance. On the move, however, the impression changed to amazement that he remained upright at all. Clumsy and nimble in the same motion, JJ had a knack for being both too fast for his own good and too slow to get out of the way. Blessed with strong bones and a particularly hard head, he seemed impervious to injury no matter the speed at impact or density of the object.

As with horses the standard measuring point of height for dogs is the withers, the ridge at the base of the neck between the shoulder blades. Most fully grown bloodhounds reach twenty-five to twenty-seven inches. Furniture makers and interior decorators will note that this range reaches quite close to the average height of dining tables: twenty-eight to thirty inches. Anyone thinking the food is safe by mere inches would be forgetting to account for the dog's neck and head, which comfortably pivots another eight to ten inches above the withers. You might as well set a place at the table for your bloodhound.

• • •

By his first birthday, JJ's height was beginning to match the early promise of his paws, but he still had a way to go in both muscular and mental maturity. But however much of a handful he was, JJ still made for a welcome relief for Serio when he returned home from a long day at work. Only four months out of the police academy when he got JJ, Serio was still a rookie by any estimation. He worked as a patrol officer during the day shift and learned quickly that his days on duty rarely, if ever, panned out like an episode of *CSI*.

Serio chose to become a police officer for a number of reasons. The father of a friend in middle school was an FBI agent, and young Serio thought that was cool. His own father was in the Special Forces and had served in the military in Vietnam and during Serio's entire childhood. Big brother Joe, however, probably influenced him the most—though not so much in the style with which he pursued it. Older by four years, Joe was a kick-ass-and-take-names police officer in Austin, Texas. He had a commanding presence in a police uniform, and the criminal element feared him. When applying for jobs, Serio was offered a position with the Austin PD, but his brother had always told him: "Do as I say, not as I do." Joe had blazed a path, so Serio knew which routes not to take. As much as he loved and respected his brother, Serio decided to go his own way.

At first Serio usually responded to burglary calls, of a car or house. He saw where the thief had broken the window and entered the premises, noted the damage inside, and catalogued the stolen items as reported by the victim. Each time Serio sympathetically tried to make the victims feel that the police were doing everything they could, that they would try to catch the

JJ's height was beginning to match the early promise of his paws, but he still had a way to go in both muscular and mental maturity.

Photograph courtesy of Mike and Lisa Serio

person or people responsible and recover the stolen property. But Serio soon discovered that all he was doing was documenting. "You had your diamond earrings stolen, your grandmother's pass-me-down plate, your computer, stereo, power drill . . . " He was putting it all on paper that made it into the hands of detectives, but the chances of solving the crime hovered in the neighborhood of 3 percent or less. After a week or so had passed with no results, many of the victims called Serio asking about any updates. He had to tell them that the police had closed the case because they didn't have any leads.

Serio imagined what it would be like if someone broke into his house and took his valuables, possibly with his family at home. Every cop in the world wanted to help on a call in progress and catch the perpetrator. But that didn't happen too often during the day shift. Taking dictation in the wake of a crime comprised the bulk of Serio's workday. Then he went home, took JJ for a walk, and time after time watched him pick up a scent and go. At first he thought it was just a neat trick. Then he thought, *Maybe there's something to this.*

Serio knew of the bloodhound's reputation as a good tracker, but as he repeatedly returned from days spent documenting stolen property to see JJ's innate skills in the park, he wondered why nobody had them working for the Salt Lake City PD or, as he soon discovered, the entire state of Utah.

JJ was intended to be a pet only. Serio had no designs on being a K9 officer. He knew that for him and JJ it was both too early and too late. Too early because he was still a relatively new patrol officer and wouldn't even be considered for a Special Squad position like K9 for at least another two to three years. Too late because JJ was already over a year old, and professional tracking dogs begin training at the significantly more impressionable age of eight weeks.

But JJ kept showing off. Even to Serio's untrained eye, it was clear that JJ's nose was remarkable. He imagined what JJ could do with a little formal training. Maybe, if JJ got good enough, Serio could show the police department what his dog could do. JJ's skills would perfectly showcase a bloodhound's potential usefulness. The idea was far-fetched, but Serio decided to have fun with JJ while he explored it. If they succeeded and the Salt Lake City Police Department got a bloodhound of their own—all the better.

Serio and JJ started to train.

• • •

JJ had a gift. No longer a worthy opponent for JJ during hide-and-seek in the house, Serio had to step it up a notch. But where to begin? Serio's dog training skills didn't extend much beyond potty training. By 1998 the Internet as we know it today was taking shape, but it hadn't yet become the primary source of information for a large segment of society. Serio turned to the Yellow Pages and, just after the section on schools, found the word *Schutzhund*.

German for "protection dog," *Schutzhund* developed in Germany in the early 1900s to test and enhance the workability of German shepherds. The sport grew in popularity, opened to other breeds, and spread to America. Established in 1979, the United Schutzhund Clubs of America, the largest organization of its kind in the United States, has member clubs throughout the country. One happened to lie just a few miles from Serio's home.

Schutzhund training develops courage, intelligence, protective instinct, ability to scent, endurance, and obedience, with those traits evaluated in their competitions. It all sounded pretty good to Serio, so he signed JJ up. As a puppy JJ had gone to obedience and socialization classes, but Schutzhund training lay in an entirely different realm. JJ was the only bloodhound there, which wasn't a problem because he was used to being a minority, and the German shepherds, Belgian Malinois, Dobermans, and rottweilers all seemed welcoming enough.

The mood changed, however, when the trainer, a short man with thinning hair and a thick mustache, stood in the middle of the dogs with a bamboo stick in one hand and a large padded sleeve made of jute wrapped around his other arm. He aggressively swung the stick, yelling at the dogs, inciting them to violence. He wanted them to bite him. They all took the bait—growling, barking, snapping, and lunging before biting down hard on the sleeve and shaking their heads, thrashing back and forth. All except for JJ. He just lay on the ground and watched the spectacle, looking for all the world as if a thought bubble were floating over his head, asking, "What on earth am I doing here?" Serio wondered the same.

When Serio had a chance to get the trainer aside, he told him about JJ's natural tracking ability, confessed that he didn't know what he was doing, and asked about teaching techniques. In a separate session the trainer took Serio out into a field and explained the principles of teaching a dog to track. Then he demonstrated how to lay a track for JJ. He started by stomping his feet in the grass and then dropped a bunch of hot dogs. Next he took a step, stomped the grass, and dropped a hot dog. Took a step, stomped the grass, dropped a hot dog. He repeated the procedure over a distance of about forty yards. Baffled, Serio prepared JJ to run the track.

JJ put his nose down and ate all the hot dogs in the initial scent path. Then he ran full speed to the end of the track, ate the last hot dog, and worked his way back, eating all the hot dogs he had passed along the way. It was the last Schutzhund training session that JJ attended. The only thing he took away from the experience was some delicious hot dogs, which he had never eaten before, and a horrible case of gas that stunk up the whole house.

Serio looked for other resources. A tip from a fellow officer led to the National Police Bloodhound Association. Established in 1966, the NPBA is based and largely focused on the East Coast, where bloodhounds, though still rare in police departments, have had a more established history with law enforcement. Serio wasn't using JJ on the job or for search and rescue, so he didn't meet the membership requirements. But he did order an old NPBA handbook from 1977 called the *Police Pocket Training Manual for Bloodhound Handlers*. Serio studied it carefully and began to apply its training methods.

Serio drove out to the hospital grounds or a public park and left JJ in the car while he walked a long, winding loop. He crossed a variety of terrain—grassy fields, bushes, sidewalks, parking lots—periodically setting down treats. Serio then got JJ out of the car, leashed him up, scented him at the start, and followed. Nose like a vacuum inhaling the ground, JJ retraced the loop from beginning to end. Serio, knowing the right and wrong turns, studied JJ's body language while tracking. Being able to read your dog accurately, to know how he acts on and off the scent, is critical. When JJ was on, he carried his tail high and curled, wagging with excitement. At a crossing of the scent trail, he gave a quick head pop, swung his nose left and right, dug in his feet, bayed emphatically, and lunged toward his goal, pulling Serio along in powerful jerks.

To mark the end of a track, Serio left a large pile of treats and gave heaps of high-pitched praise and heavy petting. Imagine

"Who's a good boy?!" with five shots of espresso taken to a national cheerleading competition. JJ ate up the treats and boisterous praise in equal measure.

Tracking yourself is useful for finding that missing set of keys but not much else. Serio next enlisted help. He turned to the other love of his life, Lisa. Together since their sophomore year in high school in Northern Virginia, they rarely spent time apart for more than single-digit hours. George Mason University recruited Serio to play soccer after he graduated from high school, while Lisa attended the University of Mary Washington, a one-hour drive away. The distance proved too great. After their freshman year, they both transferred to Virginia Tech, where Serio continued to play NCAA Division I soccer and Lisa began a path that would lead to an MBA and a tolerance for Serio's quirks that bordered on a state of Zen.

"It's important that you listen," Serio told her at the start of a tracking session. "I need you to go across the field and straight to that tree, make a right, and go until you get to those trash cans." Lisa left a hat or glove on the ground as a scent article, set off as instructed, and found a spot to hide. Serio waited about twenty minutes for the scent trail to age a bit, then started JJ on the track. JJ would be doing well, showing a high drive and following directly along the path Serio specified for Lisa. Then he turned right where Serio knew he should have gone left. Serio waited for JJ to correct his mistake, but the dog kept pulling to the right. Frustrated, Serio pulled JJ back to the missed turn and guided him to the left. Obliging to a point, JJ went left for a little bit, lost interest in that direction, then insisted on going back to the right. After a few more corrections, Serio finally gave up and let JJ go where he wanted. Nose to the ground and tail in the air, JJ led Serio directly to Lisa's hiding spot.

"I told you to go left," Serio immediately said to Lisa, still on the ground in a cramped hiding spot, trying to get up while a big bloodhound leapt on her with large muddy paws and slobbered all over her face.

"You did not. You said right."

The argument continued. Only JJ was happy. Serio and Lisa fought all the way back home.

"I'm never going to set a track for you again," Lisa said. She said this about 70 percent of the time. All told, she set well over a hundred tracks for JJ. Like any couple worth their salt, the arguments continued, but so did the love.

When Serio and Lisa were married a year to the day after getting JJ, the big hound took part in the event. Leashed to a tree at the top of a hill during the outdoor ceremony, JJ was in the nosebleed section, but he could still hear the proceedings well enough. Johann Sebastian Bach didn't write the Ariosa for Cantata no. 156 with an arrangement for a bloodhound, but that didn't stop JJ from baying along as the wedding processional began. JJ lent his voice to the music, and it sounded all the sweeter. He bayed at other moments throughout the ceremony, but when asked to "Speak now or forever hold" his peace, he held it.

4

WRINKLE

The head is furnished with an amount of loose skin, which in nearly every position appears superabundant, but more particularly so when the head is carried low; the skin then falls into loose, pendulous ridges and folds, especially over the forehead and sides of the face.

August 1998

As he matured JJ's training grew a little more sophisticated. No longer just following the smells of known family members, JJ began tracking friends, neighbors, and anyone else willing to lend their smell and lie in wait for a big bloodhound to come lick them with gusto. A group of young volunteers from the local Boy Scout troop often eagerly helped out. Adam Childs, a thirteen-year-old with a high tolerance for slobber, was JJ's most frequent quarry at the time.

Although he was a Boy Scout, you wouldn't have seen a kid like Adam on any of their recruitment posters. He wore his hair long and bleached it blond; multiple earrings dangled from his lobes, and he sported heavy-soled Doc Martens, fashionable combat boots with distinctive yellow stitching and a required part of the uniform for membership in a subculture that despises uniformity. The oldest of four, Adam didn't particularly care for his stepfather's constant presence, wanting his real dad around instead. In a short time Serio became the first solid male influence that Adam acknowledged. For his part Serio saw a good kid who wanted to be around JJ as much as he could, thrilled just to be a part of the training team.

On Adam's first time out with Serio and JJ, they walked to a park near Adam's house. Serio gave Adam an old T-shirt that he rubbed on his arms, neck, and head to transfer his scent. Serio explained what he wanted him to do. Adam recalls that day as though it were yesterday.

"He had me go out and do some zigzags and some crazy turns, go straight, walk out, come back, cross-track my path, and find a good hiding spot. I remember I found my spot in between these two little hills, and the whole time I was just lying there excited because I could hear JJ just howling, like he wanted it.

JJ on a training track, nose to the ground, tail in the air, hot on the trail.
Photograph courtesy of Mike and Lisa Serio

That was one of the coolest things to me. I had that opportunity to be found for the first time."

Every few weeks, whenever Serio could break away and needed a reliable runner to lay a track, he called Adam, and off they went to some new park or field so JJ could fine-tune his nasal sorcery. JJ got better with each training run. Serio liked what he saw, as did Adam and the other volunteers. What Serio needed now was an expert to take a look. He decided that the best way to showcase JJ's talents was to shoot a video. Lisa worked the camera, a neighbor laid a track, and he and JJ did their thing.

Aesthetically, the video leaves much to be desired and not just because JJ's backside was the featured view. Filmed the same year as *The Blair Witch Project*, the video had a similar choppy, nausea-inducing quality best viewed from the corner of your eye and with a dose of Dramamine at the ready. The sound quality was pretty good, although that wasn't necessarily a point in the video's favor. You can hear every breath Lisa takes as she tries to follow a fast-moving target and keep the camera, if not steady, at least pointed in the right direction. Serio added to Lisa's inhale-exhale harmony by telling JJ, "Good boy!" every three seconds or so. Thank goodness, JJ proved himself a natural showman. Even with the less than stellar direction, cinematography, and soundtrack, the video highlighted its star's unbeatable mix of confidence and charisma that audiences can't resist.

• • •

Sergeant Don Campbell had a deep voice and a strict, by-the-book veteran's toughness. Serio remembers nights when Sergeant Campbell covered the graveyard shift and tore Serio's field reports apart, emphatically pointing out any error, inconsistency, or missed detail. It was the kind of stern treatment Serio had expected when he joined the force, and Campbell delivered. Approaching the sergeant with a jittery video of JJ in hand wasn't easy, but Campbell headed the K9 Squad.

The Salt Lake City K9 Squad consisted of five German shepherds and a handler for each dog, all experienced officers with a minimum of five years on the force. Taken together, the group made for a whole lot of teeth and testosterone. The K9 teams responded to all manner of requests for their services, including finding explosives and firearms, but primarily, they sniffed out narcotics and apprehended criminals who either fled from the police or fought them. Tracking humans beyond a contained building or block didn't lie beyond the realm of possibility for the department's patrol dogs, but it was unusual. They didn't attempt anything much farther than two blocks, however. So when Serio told Campbell stories about his pet bloodhound tracking long distances over urban terrain, the sergeant was understandably a little dubious. Determined, Serio convinced him to watch the video.

Although Campbell didn't know bloodhounds well, he had been working with patrol dogs for nearly two decades. He knew that a dog's performance in training can differ greatly from how he performs in the uncontrolled chaos of a real-world scenario. Nevertheless, what he saw intrigued him. JJ's abilities were crystal clear. A stickler for proper procedure, Campbell said he couldn't do much for Serio since he wasn't his supervisor. If Serio wanted to pursue his bloodhound idea further, Campbell suggested that he talk to his patrol sergeant.

Everybody liked Sergeant Chris Burbank. He had been Serio's firearms instructor in the police academy and, with his professional but easygoing personality, acted as a buffer between the more militaristic, no-nonsense academy instructors and the young cadets struggling to enter a new world that had its own language, rules, and unwritten code of conduct. One day during academy training, Serio was matched up against Burbank in a timed competition. The object of the contest was to sprint sixty yards; assemble the frame, recoil spring, barrel, slide, and ammunition clip of a Glock 17 handgun; and shoot five steel plates the size of human heads and five upper body silhouettes positioned fifteen yards away.

"Oh shit, I got Serio," Burbank said, knowing that the young cadet was renowned as the fastest runner of his class. Burbank and Serio lined up and took off at the sound of a whistle. Serio beat Burbank to the unassembled gun with time to spare, but Burbank had worked as a member of the Special Weapons and Tactics (SWAT) team for years and was, after all, the academy firearms instructor. Serio didn't stand a chance.

Officers young and old felt comfortable talking to Burbank about most anything, a trait that proved particularly important eight years down the road when he took up an appointment as the chief of police, Salt Lake City's youngest in history. In 1998, however, Burbank was a graveyard-shift sergeant assigned to Serio's patrol division. Burbank looked at the video, similarly impressed. He asked Serio what kind of training he'd done with JJ. Serio told him about the Schutzhund training fiasco and what he'd learned on his own from books and trial and error. Burbank suggested that he take it a step further and find more specialized training elsewhere. The department couldn't pay for it, but if Serio could find an appropriate training seminar, Burbank would make sure that none of his vacation days would be used up while he attended.

It felt like progress. Serio could train with JJ and count it as a workday. Unfortunately, an upcoming bloodhound seminar held in Illinois was full. All the dog spots were taken, but Serio could attend as an observer. Leaving JJ behind, Serio went to Illinois, but he didn't go empty-handed. He brought his brilliantly amateur video of JJ, determined to show it to anybody who'd watch.

Salem, Illinois, lays claim to fame as the birthplace of William Jennings Bryan, the three-time presidential loser and one-time winner for the prosecution in *Tennessee vs. John Thomas Scopes*, better known as the Scopes Monkey Trial. Salem's second claim to fame is its disputed contention as the home of Miracle Whip salad dressing. (The headquarters of Kraft Foods in Northfield, Illinois, also claims credit for the concoction.) It's also a great place for bloodhounds. Jack Shuler, a retired K9 officer and certified instructor for the National Police Bloodhound Association, has bred, trained, and worked with bloodhounds in Salem for more than thirty-five years. A former trailing trial judge for the American Bloodhound Club, he is one of the world's foremost experts in training bloodhounds for both police work and search and rescue.

K9 handlers far and wide came to Salem to participate in Shuler's Mantrailing seminars. For this group Serio's trek from Utah was easily the farthest. Over three unseasonably cold days in early November, Serio listened, took notes, asked questions, and followed behind other handlers and their dogs as they ran scent trails through Salem's parks and in the woods just outside the city. Serio absorbed every scrap of bloodhound knowledge thrown his way. It helped him acquire a lot of useful knowledge in a short time, but he also absorbed a lot of bullshit. It took Serio a few years of experience to shake some of the stronger opinions spouted as facts bantered about during any large gathering of bloodhound handlers. Everybody had his or her own ideas about how bloodhounds scent and what they can and can't do.

Being without JJ was hard, but the chance to observe and talk about dogs all day and night with fellow officers offered a new thrill. Still believing that he had started JJ too late to consider him for active police duty, Serio took heart that, in his estimation, JJ could do just about everything the other dogs were doing. But no experienced handler had seen JJ in action. After three days of watching other dogs, Serio couldn't stand it any longer. On the last night of the seminar, Shuler invited all the participants to his house for a barbecue. Serio brought the video and waited to find the perfect time. He didn't find it, so he asked anyway. Shuler didn't really want to watch the video but acquiesced nonetheless. Other handlers gathered around the television to watch. Shuler chuckled when he first saw JJ onscreen and said something about him not looking like a "real" bloodhound.

What Shuler meant by that comment goes to the heart of a controversy in the bloodhound world. JJ had a lot of wrinkles compared to your average dog but not compared to other blood-hounds. JJ was beautiful, as anyone with taste could see, but his physical features wouldn't win him many points at the Westminster Kennel Club. He wasn't a show dog. Shuler firmly believed that the best trailing bloodhounds came from bloodlines that best matched the breed standards defined by the Kennel Club of the United Kingdom and the American Kennel Club. The best mantrailer best fit the bloodhound mold.

Other bloodhound experts believe the opposite, that inbreed-ing within bloodhound show dogs, where size and shape have such importance, has not only resulted in a higher frequency of health issues, such as heart problems and hip dysplasia, but it also has corrupted the dog's drive and scenting ability on the trail. The dogs without show quality characteristics, sometimes called working line bloodhounds by breeders, are generally smaller, less wrinkled, and healthier, making them the better trackers—or so the belief goes. Still others believe that a bloodhound's trailing ability cannot be determined by looks alone and that the controversy is just silly. Serio didn't know enough to have an opinion on the matter at the time, but he later came around to the latter point of view.

Sitting in Shuler's living room that evening, already feeling that he had overstepped his host's good graces, Serio kept his mouth shut and let the video do the talking. Best in show or not, JJ's talents couldn't be denied. Shuler and the other handlers were paying attention. When the video ended, Shuler didn't say much, but Serio could tell that JJ had made an impression. An experienced search-and-rescue handler in the group noted JJ's boisterous and frequent bay while on the trail and let Serio know just how rare that was in modern bloodhounds. She explained that the trait is more of a pack hound behavior, seen in foxhounds and beagles, and was common in earlier bloodhounds, but the breed has largely lost that trait over the generations. A few bloodhounds bay at the start of a trail, eager to get going, and often when they find their quarry at trail's end, but most generally run pretty quiet the rest of the time. JJ bayed at the beginning, the end, and at all the turns in between. The search-and-rescue handler told Serio that he'd have one of the best trailing dogs ever.

When Serio returned to Utah, he no longer wanted to train in obscurity and beg for an audience to watch his video. He had to get JJ in the flesh in front of experienced bloodhound handlers.

There were no bloodhound training seminars scheduled soon enough, so he called the number listed at the back of the 1977 NPBA bloodhound training manual that he had been carrying around with him everywhere he went.

Like Jack Shuler, Bill Tolhurst was a law enforcement officer and a widely regarded K9 instructor. He was also a legend, considered by many the father of modern bloodhound trailing in law enforcement. Thrice past president of the NPBA, Tolhurst had authored many books and training manuals on bloodhounds and invented the STU-100, a device that looked not unlike the ghost-sucking machine used by Bill Murray's Peter Venkman and his partners in *Ghostbusters*. The Scent Transfer Unit collected trace scent evidence at a crime scene without contamination and allowed law enforcement to store the evidence in scent banks for future use on repeat offenders.

From puppy training to the equipment used to maximize trailing techniques, scent dogs were Tolhurst's passion, occupying both his professional and recreational pursuits. He believed that every handler should silently repeat the phrase, "I believe my dog!" before starting a trail. "When you start trying to outthink your dog and run the trail for him," Tolhurst wrote, "take the harness off the dog, send him home, and put it on yourself."

Tolhurst loved to talk about bloodhounds. When Serio called him and started asking questions, Tolhurst gave generously of his time and knowledge. They talked bloodhounds at length. Tolhurst lived in upstate New York, so he suggested that Serio contact his long-time work partner, Larry Harris, who lived in California and knew the K9 community in the West more intimately.

"Come on out to California," said Harris to Serio. "A few of us are getting together to train." Harris had never met Serio before,

Mike, Lisa, and JJ with Larry Harris's bloodhound, Trace, at the beach in Santa Barbara where JJ had fun chasing seagulls.
Photograph courtesy of Mike and Lisa Serio

but the police bloodhound clan is small, and Harris was happy to share his expertise with a prospective member—even one not yet directly affiliated with a police K9 program.

While Burbank had given Serio flexibility with counting bloodhound training as work days, the extra time to drive out and back from California would be too much. He had to fly. But a fully grown bloodhound significantly exceeds even the most lenient airline's carry-on luggage size limit. Service dogs for the blind and dogs traveling for law enforcement or search-and-rescue operations generally can fly in the cabin no matter their size, but JJ wasn't any of these. He was a police officer's pet. Oliver Wendell Holmes once said, "Young men know the rules, but old men know the exceptions." Harris told Serio to get a search-and-rescue vest and put it on JJ. For additional cover, Sergeant Campbell wrote a letter for Serio to carry with him stating that he was transporting JJ to attend a law enforcement training seminar. No one asked to see it.

Larry Harris had worked for many years as a K9 officer for the Irvine Police Department and coinvented the Scent Transfer Unit with Bill Tolhurst. His expertise with bloodhounds was well known, and he had trained a number of police handlers and their bloodhounds. Serio and JJ were in capable hands. Harris had also invited two civilian search-and-rescue bloodhound handlers to train near his house in Santa Barbara, making Serio the greenest of the group by far.

JJ had never formally trained beyond Serio's diligent but amateur efforts, so Harris started them from the beginning. He pretended that the full-grown JJ was a puppy and showed Serio how to train a dog with no tracking experience. Puppy training involves a lot more food rewards than normal, so JJ didn't mind. Nor did Serio, thrilled to be getting a solid foundation for bloodhound training from an experienced handler who could give him direct feedback and answer his questions.

After the puppy runs, Harris laid longer trails for JJ and eventually moved to trails across paved surfaces using chalk to indicate the direction he'd gone. The markers gave the handlers better reads on their dogs at critical points on the trail. Lisa followed behind Serio and JJ with a walkie-talkie, periodically relaying updates of their progress to Harris.

It was all a lot of fun for JJ, but his happiest moment there had nothing to do with training. Serio and Lisa had rented a room at a Motel 6 near the beach. After a day of being leashed to his harness, JJ ran free and chased seagulls until he flopped over, too tired to move. He had never seen the birds before and was determined to catch one. They often waited until the last minute, then lifted up into the air, just out of reach, only to settle back down on the shoreline a few yards away. JJ bayed at them over and over, but the seagulls had heard similar protests from sea lions and harbor seals that voiced their displeasure whenever the birds swooped in to steal their food.

Harris strongly advised Serio not to let JJ chase the gulls again, however. He believed that bloodhounds shouldn't get positive reinforcement when pursuing anything other than humans. Learning to associate chasing animals with fun might make the dog more distractible on the trail, lowering his drive to follow human scent. All along, Serio listened and learned. But with the seagulls he made an exception. He felt that JJ could distinguish between play and work. Harness on, clipped to a leash, and a "Ready to go to *work?*" meant business. Leash off in the woods or at the beach meant go nuts; enjoy the perks of being a big, fast dog without a care in the world.

EARS

The ears are thin and soft to the touch, extremely long, set very low, and fall in graceful folds, the lower parts curling inwards and backwards.

September 1998

Nancy Palmer had last spoken with her ten-year-old daughter, Anna, when the child called to ask for permission to play with some friends. Two hours later Nancy found Anna lying on their front porch in a pool of blood, her face waxy and pale. Her daughter's hand felt cold to the touch, so she frantically called 9-1-1. The emergency dispatcher instructed Nancy to begin CPR. It wasn't working, though, because her daughter had a hole in her throat. The dispatcher told Nancy to put her hand over the hole and try again.

The paramedics arrived within minutes—an eternity for any parent under the circumstances. The ambulance transported Anna to the hospital, where doctors pronounced her dead. They noted the bruises on her chest and face and also evidence of sexual assault. One wound pierced her spinal cord, an injury that would have paralyzed her from the chest down, had another stab wound not severed her jugular vein, causing her to bleed to death.

Salt Lake City police detectives learned details of the last hours of Anna's life from another ten-year-old, her friend Loxane Konesavanh. The two girls had walked to 7-Eleven to buy gum, played on the swings at the park, and peeked into Loxane's sister's bedroom to catch a glimpse of the *MTV Music Awards*. The girls then walked to a street corner halfway between their houses where they normally parted company. Loxane recounted that they stopped at the corner to let a man walking behind them pass. When they did, he looked at Anna. Loxane worried that the man might kidnap them. Anna told her to run home. Loxane did, and that was the last time she saw her friend. Another witness, a fourteen-year-old, saw a man walking near the two girls that evening, but the description of the suspect didn't match Loxane's.

Although the crime must have occurred sometime during the evening rush hour and near a busy intersection, investigators found the lack of witnesses frustrating. Extensive media coverage, including a segment on *America's Most Wanted*, and an eleven-thousand-dollar reward for information turned up numerous leads. The police pursued over a thousand leads, but none led to an arrest. The case went cold.

Lieutenant Mike Roberts had seen the horrific crime scene. He—like the chief of police, patrol officers, crime lab technicians, and everyone else involved—wanted to be able to tell the victim's family and the public that the SLCPD was doing everything possible, a desire never truer than in the brutal murder of a child. When investigators have nothing to show for their efforts, frustration turns to anger and despair. So a few months later, when a rookie officer in Lieutenant Roberts's patrol division approached him with an unusual idea, he thought it might be worth trying. Mike Serio suggested introducing a bloodhound to the Salt Lake City Police K9 Squad. Lieutenant Roberts wasn't sure what kind of success a bloodhound team could deliver, if any, but he thought of Anna Palmer.

The tracking video had interested Serio's patrol sergeant enough to allow him time to seek training without burning vacation days. Serio's reports on how JJ was doing in training kept the K9 sergeant intrigued. In the police hierarchy, however, it's a long way from sergeant to chief, and as in most public organizations, the bureaucracy train can be slow or fail to arrive at the desired destination. Convincing Lieutenant Roberts was a step in the right direction, but many levels remained between a droopy-eared K9 dream and reality.

Captain Scott Folsom, head of the Liberty Patrol Division, which covers the east side of Salt Lake City, stood next up the chain. He also oversaw the K9 Squad. At the time the standard depiction of the dogs in movies colored Folsom's ideas of police bloodhounds. "It seemed like it was always a good ol' boy Southern sheriff who had the good ol' boy hounds," said Folsom, before breaking into a mock Southern accent. "'Y'all go in the thicket and get 'em, Bubba!'"

"Put that aside," said Serio, explaining to Folsom how bloodhounds were trained and how their purpose differed from that of patrol dogs such as German shepherds. He also described ways that police departments in other parts of the country, primarily on the East Coast and in the South, were using the animals. But even in these more bloodhound-friendly regions, the police bloodhound still remains a rarity.

Shaun Hopkins, a reserve officer with the Jack County Sheriff's Department in north-central Texas, called bloodhounds "the most underutilized tool in law enforcement." She volunteered her time and the talents of her bloodhound, Ashley, to help track evidence and people for the Dallas, Lancaster, and Carrollton police departments as well as for the Texas Rangers. "You hear a lot of times that 'we've done everything possible,'" she said. "Until you use a professional bloodhound team, you haven't."

Citing the Anna Palmer case and its lack of leads, Lieutenant Roberts also worked on convincing Captain Folsom, listing other potential applications he saw for a bloodhound in scenarios police officers more routinely encountered. K9 Sergeant Campbell had shown interest, advising Serio to follow the chain of command; Sergeant Burbank had given the green light to explore the idea with outside training; and Lieutenant Roberts was backing the idea for a bloodhound recruitment.

Folsom could see Serio's undeniable yet respectful persistence and was open to the idea, but he understood the department's hierarchy well and knew that funding would be an issue. Dogs cost money. The dogs themselves are expensive to start, but the real cost comes from training both dog and handler, medical care, food, and equipment, in particular custom-designed police vehicles that require an aluminum kennel insert and a climate-controlled system for the dog in Salt Lake's extreme fluctuations in temperature, from one-hundred-degree–plus summer days to winter nights well below freezing. Police budgets were shrinking, staffing shortages were a constant concern, and the police department was preparing for the 2002 Winter Olympics. Folsom told Serio to get to work on a presentation, and he'd run it up the chain. But he knew the money for it just wasn't there.

Serio enlisted his friends and got to work. Matt Larsen had gone through the police academy with Serio. The two men graduated at the top of their class, first and second respectively. The brains of the duo, Matt later left the force to become a medical doctor specializing in emergency medicine. Serio, who always felt inferior in the academic arena, not just to Matt but to nearly everyone, scored well on tests because he worked hard. Much smarter than he'd ever acknowledge, he found his real strength, however, in athletics. A scholarship athlete in college and winner of the physical fitness award for both the state and city police academies, he could bench press twice his weight and, in the words of his former sergeant, "run like a cheetah."

Lee Dobrowolski, later a deputy chief, repeatedly told the story of running with Serio after two young guys seen breaking into cars. Serio caught up to the first one and tackled him to the ground. Dobrowolski was still chasing the other one when Serio, seeing Dobrowolski getting winded, yelled, "Come here, and hold this guy!" Dobrowolski gladly did so while Serio sprinted off and caught the other thief.

With the brashness of youth and less than two years' experience working as patrol officers, Larsen and Serio, with a whole lot of help from Lisa, put together a proposal to expand Salt Lake City's K9 program, adding two German shepherds to the current five and one floppy-eared bloodhound. Larsen found grant money that they believed would address at least a part of the funding issue and help increase their chances of approval.

The K9 sergeant supported the proposal but expected the brass to go only for the German shepherd expansion, probably agreeing to add only one dog. He was right about the one dog—but wrong about the breed. After taking counsel from the chief, Captain Scott Folsom, with a nod from Lieutenant Roberts, denied the German shepherd proposal and agreed to the bloodhound.

Excited, Serio had achieved his improbable goal: The Salt Lake City Police Department was going to get a bloodhound of its own. The K9 Squad could now buy a bloodhound puppy, train the dog with input from Serio, and have one of the existing K9 officers run the bloodhound when the dog was ready for police work. Serio for his part could put in for a position with the SWAT Team, the unit sergeant of which had already been recruiting him. Serio always expected to wind up in SWAT. The position played to his physical strengths: athleticism and a compact frame, both good for storming through windows.

But Serio, after all his efforts, felt that he and JJ had been cut out of the loop. He also worried about existing K9 officers running the new bloodhound. Other than Sergeant Campbell, they hadn't shown much enthusiasm for the idea in the first place. Assigning a skeptical German shepherd handler wasn't the right way to begin.

But Serio couldn't do much about the decision, so he and JJ got out of town for a few days. They headed to California's Bay Area for the first Golden State Bloodhound Seminar, sponsored by the Alameda Police Department. Police and search-and-rescue dogs from agencies across the country were going there to train. Serio and JJ didn't plan to miss it.

HEAD

The head is narrow in proportion to its length, and long in proportion to the body, tapering but slightly from the temples to the end of the muzzle. The length from end of nose to stop (midway between the eyes) should be not less than that from stop to back of occipital protuberance (peak). The entire length of head from the posterior part of the peak to the end of the muzzle should be 12 inches, or more.

April 1999

Oakland in the springtime can feel a lot like Beirut—at least in terms of the weather. When it comes to personal safety, however, you'd be much better off in Lebanon's capital city. With a violent crime rate of more than fifteen incidents per one thousand people, Oakland ranks as California's most dangerous city. Throw in property crimes such as burglary, larceny, and vehicle theft, and your average Oakland resident has a one in sixteen chance of being a crime victim, not in his or her lifetime but *every single year*. For bloodhounds that just means a lot of bad guys to smell.

Jeff Schettler, a young K9 officer and rising star in the very small police bloodhound community, hosted the Golden State Bloodhound Seminar held in Oakland that April. What he lacked in years of experience, he made up for with gumption and organizational skills. The event included a large roster of people, balanced more or less equally between police officers and search-and-rescue handlers, and of course dogs.

Despite "bloodhound" in the seminar title, a number of other breeds, including German shepherds and rottweilers, crashed the party. The mix might bring to mind one of those insufferable word problems on an algebra exam: *Betty Sue counted 195 heads and 570 legs at the bloodhound seminar. Assuming each person has 2 legs and each dog has 4, how many people and how many dogs were there?* (See "Notes and Sources" at the back of the book to check your work.)

Serio and JJ, who added two heads and six legs to the total, had a chance to meet more of the *Who's Who* of the law enforcement bloodhound community. Larry Harris, who also mentored Schettler, attended, as did K9 instructors John Lutenberg, a renowned expert from Colorado, and Jerry Nichols, another experienced Colorado trainer better known as the K9 handler of

Yogi. Although he had died the year before, Yogi was perhaps the nation's most famous bloodhound, featured on *Unsolved Mysteries* after he helped locate the body of a five-year-old four days after she was abducted.

The seminar began like any other with introductions and PowerPoint presentations. It could as easily have been an annual meeting of the American Society of Colon and Rectal Surgeons or Allergy Sufferers Anonymous—if not for the dog hair on everyone's jeans. After preliminaries dog teams split up among the instructors, and everybody went to work. The cadaver dogs went for a swim in the harbor at the Alameda Naval Air Station. Never a big fan of the water, JJ wasn't envious. He was not fond of looking for dead pigs immersed in the harbor to simulate the smell of decomposed drowning victims; neither was Serio. They headed to drier pastures to work on trailing techniques in urban environments.

Even though the seminar lasted three days, handlers only had a few chances to run their dogs. Serio and JJ had to make the most of it. On the last day they ran a long, challenging track. Jerry Nichols instructed Serio and followed them closely, as did a few other handlers, one a federal agent wearing a vest with "US Marshal" emblazoned all over it. The track started in Alameda and led over the bridge into Oakland. Serio worried that JJ might shut down on the bridge because the walking path, made entirely of steel, reverberated with strange sounds. Also, like many other animals, canine and otherwise, JJ usually didn't like standing on anything see-through. Serio needn't have worried. JJ stuck his nose on the hard surface, bayed, and took off.

When they crossed the bridge, Serio thought it looked just like what he'd seen on cop shows depicting the most dangerous part of town: industrial buildings, commercial property littered with graffiti of questionable grammar, piles of trash, broken bottles, rusted metal, and groups of hardened men huddling in the corners. JJ continued pulling and baying, and Serio's entourage of lawmen followed at his heels. The guys huddled on the Oakland side looked up and then looked at one another, no doubt wondering, *What the hell is going on?* They didn't stick around to find out, though. They scattered—some at a quick jog and others in an all-out sprint. JJ didn't pay them any attention. He had someone else's scent in mind. Along sidewalks, across streets, and over dirt and gravel, JJ sniffed and nailed his turns with the confidence of a seasoned pro. He found his mark hiding behind a building, released a few final emphatic bays, and earned his reward of praise, pets, and tasty doggie treats.

Nichols, one of the nation's most celebrated bloodhound handlers, was very impressed. "You've got a good dog," he said to Serio. "JJ's going to be a real good dog."

Serio returned to Utah brimming with confidence but more frustrated than ever, knowing that his role in Salt Lake's new bloodhound program wouldn't go beyond consultant. Leaving JJ at home each day, he returned to his regular patrol duties on the graveyard shift for another week. Then he and JJ boarded another plane, this time to Maryland for a seminar sponsored by the National Police Bloodhound Association. Jack Shuler, Weldon Wood, Doug Lowry, and a bevy of other experienced East Coast instructors attended, as did over a hundred handlers and their bloodhounds. After three days following behind JJ as he sniffed, bayed, and slobbered on his finds, Serio knew his dog was one of the best, a belief no doubt shared by many other handlers about their own dogs. JJ indisputably made the most noise, though. None of the other hundred or so dogs bayed as often or as flamboyantly as he did.

When Serio returned from Maryland, he didn't have any other bloodhound seminars on the horizon. He continued working his patrol shift and eagerly waited for the K9 Squad to get their puppy and start the newly approved bloodhound program. Four months passed, but nothing happened. Serio checked to see what was causing the holdup—no puppy, and no plans to get one. An insufficient budget was causing the roadblock once again. Confused, Serio thought that they'd addressed the funding issue. It would only cost the department a few hundred dollars to buy a puppy, and an existing K9 officer was going to run the dog, which meant no additional payroll and only limited equipment costs. The remaining line items of food and medical care, while not insignificant, were fairly small, and the chief of police had already approved them.

Feeling that his idea had been swept under the rug, Serio pulled it out again and made some changes. He came up with a new proposal, one brewing during the many hours he followed behind JJ as his dog smelled an invisible line of microscopic particles hovering above the ground—a line that time and again led to a would-be criminal or missing child. But this time, since the chief had approved the initial proposal, Serio felt he had a free pass to ignore the usual chain of command. He went straight to Captain Folsom.

"If we can't afford to buy a dog," Serio said, "I have a dog we can put in service. He already has some training." Serio proposed to run JJ out of his patrol car until the K9 Squad got a bloodhound of their own and trained it for deployments. That would buy him at least a year of working with JJ. Serio stressed that his new proposal would be cost neutral to the department: no new equipment, no additional pay, and no special time out for training. "I'll handle all my regular patrol duties and keep JJ in the backseat. He'll just be an extra tool to help out where he might be useful."

Folsom didn't really think a bloodhound could help catch bad guys, but he wondered how JJ might help in the search for missing persons. Several times a year the police department was sending officers out in neighborhoods and into the extensive foothills of the Salt Lake Valley looking for missing children or residents of nursing homes suffering from Alzheimer's or dementia who had wandered off.

"In my mind," Folsom said to Serio, "the biggest rationale for a bloodhound is, even if you never catch a bad guy, if you can turn the missing guy from the old folks home into a one-hour search with one or two officers versus a full-fledged neighborhood canvas, bringing in neighborhood watch and search-and-rescue people; if you don't have to walk through the foothills looking for the kid who wandered away from Mom and Dad while they were shooting off fireworks—all because the bloodhound can get them quickly recovered, well, that pays for itself pretty quickly in just the man-hours not lost."

While he certainly wanted to help find children and old folks, Serio wanted to catch bad guys with JJ even more. If budgetary savings offered the rationale for letting his dog go to work, who was he to argue? "Let's just try it and see if it works," Serio said.

Persuaded, Folsom still needed the chief's approval for the changed plan. Over the next few months, he met with an assistant chief and the chief himself a couple of times to talk about Serio's new proposal and the prospective logistics.

"Fortunately, we worked for people who weren't mired in the old way of doing business," Folsom recalled. "We were never, perhaps, the most progressive place on the planet, but from

Before the start of a track, Serio asks, "Are you ready to go to *work*?"
Photograph courtesy of Mike and Lisa Serio

time to time you have to try something new; otherwise, you stay mired in 1950."

Ultimately, after both the legal and risk-management departments dissected it, Police Chief Ruben Ortega gave the go-ahead, as long as the project was cost neutral or came out of Folsom's existing budget. *An Agreement for Use of a Bloodhound* was drawn up, citing Salt Lake City's interest "in running an experimental program to determine whether or not a bloodhound would be of use to police operations."

The department wouldn't pay extra salary or overtime, and Serio would pay for all of JJ's food and other expenses. In recognition that JJ belonged to Serio and wasn't city property, as were all the German shepherds on the K9 Squad, the department did throw him one bone that they didn't have to: "Should the dog be killed during the course of duties to Salt Lake City Corporation, the City agrees to reimburse Mike Serio the amount of $500." But the most important part of the document came last. "The parties agree that this agreement shall run for a period of 6 months. Either party may cancel the agreement upon 10 days' written notice."

Serio and JJ weren't officially joining the K9 Squad, nor were department resources headed their way, but he and JJ were getting a shot—a quick and tenuous shot, but one that Serio ecstatically took. JJ was officially a police dog.

FOREFACE

The foreface is long, deep, and of even width throughout, with square outline when seen in profile.

September 1999

JJ's start date, September 13, happily coincided with Serio's twenty-eighth birthday, right after the family's planned vacation with friends to Lake Tahoe, Serio and Lisa's favorite spot in the world.

Excellent skiers since childhood, Serio and Lisa had their first encounter with North America's largest alpine lake in the winter of 1994 on a break from college. Hooked at the first vista, they returned for summer jobs working for a parasail company. After moving to Utah, they went back to Tahoe for Serio's first vacation since becoming a Salt Lake City police officer. But this time they had a three-month-old bloodhound in tow. Serio rented a boat and took Lisa and JJ to the middle of the lake. Not fond of swimming, JJ curled up in his doggie bed on the floor of the boat. Fast asleep, he missed the action. Serio got down on one knee and proposed. Lisa, wondering why it had taken him eleven years to ask, said yes.

Fully grown on their next trip to Tahoe a year and a half later, and getting ready to begin his first day on the job as a Salt Lake City police dog, JJ still didn't like the water, but he loved to hike, particularly with his good buddy, Bear, a black German shepherd/Labrador retriever mix belonging to Devin and Kathy, Serio and Lisa's friends. Devin had gone to the police academy with Serio and had joined the West Valley Police Department, just outside Salt Lake. His wife, Kathy, was studying to be an OB/GYN.

Ridiculously in shape, all four humans were cruising up, down, and over the many scenic trails on mountain bikes. JJ and Bear ran alongside, four-legged, fast, and free. JJ darted off every now and then to chase a squirrel or gopher that he had no hope of catching. Serio heard JJ give a little whine and yelp when he picked up a scent, but Serio knew his dog would circle back around. If for some reason he didn't, Serio could signal the device on JJ's collar, giving him an audible warning to come back. Next came a mild but uncomfortable shock.

Electronic collars are standard equipment for bloodhound owners who let their dogs off leash in the woods. For even the best-trained bloodhound, the dog's drive to follow a scent to its source can overwhelm any verbal command. Fortunately, Serio didn't have to use it very often.

A little farther into the bike ride, Serio saw JJ pick up a new scent and start tracking. When JJ quickened his pace and bayed, Serio knew it wasn't a squirrel. Still riding his bike along the trail, Serio saw ahead of JJ—now in a full sprint—a large burst of black fur disappearing through the trees. The bear was at least four times JJ's size, but it had probably never heard a blood-hound bay before. JJ and Bear the dog continued in pursuit.

Serio had his handgun on him and the call box to JJ's elec-tronic collar in his backpack, but it all happened so fast that he didn't have time to get either one. The handgun, which his department encouraged him to carry even when off duty, wouldn't have been very useful against a full-grown bear any-way. Serio jumped off his bike and set off after the dogs. When he caught up with them, JJ was baying at the base of the thin-nest pine tree around. About forty feet up, the bear was swaying back and forth, looking down from the top. Branches knocked loose by the bear's ascent were falling to the ground. JJ was bay-ing; Serio was yelling at the top of his lungs calling him back; Bear the dog was barking; and the bear, easily outweighing all three, was hugging tightly to the last precarious feet of tree that touched the sky. The tree looked old, possibly dead, and much too frail. Serio worried that the bear would come crashing down at any moment. JJ finally heeded Serio's call and left the bear in peace to return to dumpster diving or whatever life of crime lay ahead.

Even though JJ had undergone extensive training under the watchful eye of some of the best experts in the business, he hadn't truly been tested. All of JJ's tracks had led to willing participants. The bear was a first. Not just for his size and species but because JJ successfully had tracked down quarry that didn't want to be found. It was the first of many to come.

• • •

Utah's first police bloodhound, an extrovert in the extreme, greeted everyone in the room with a hearty tail wag and a select few with a crotch check. After he canvassed the room to his satisfaction, he curled up in a ball at Serio's feet and quickly fell asleep. The meeting hadn't even begun.

The police lineup occurs at the start of a shift, and you've probably seen it many times on your favorite television cop show—*Hill Street Blues*, if you happen to be that old, or *CSI: Cleveland*, whenever they get around to making that one. All the jovial banter between patrol officers and their sergeant takes place, only to be interrupted by the latest updates of a serial killer on the loose or the status of a fellow officer wounded in the line of duty. A heartfelt "Be careful out there" from the sergeant dismisses them all. Salt Lake City's police lineup went exactly like that—only different. The patrol sergeant read from the Watch Command Log any significant incidents that had happened during the previous two shifts. For the graveyard shift—10:00 p.m. to 8:00 a.m.—that meant noteworthy crimes in the city since eight o'clock that morning. The majority of crimes happen late at night, so generally no more than four or five incidents make the Watch Command Log for the day and afternoon shifts.

Sergeant Dave Cracroft sat at the head of the table in the small conference room. A few ugly mug shots of Utah's most wanted criminals hung without frames on the wall behind him. About sixteen patrol officers sat close together around the table in blue plastic chairs, and one bloodhound, which Cracroft had never seen before, slept on the floor. It was an overlap night, the one night of the week when the two graveyard platoons met in the middle, one on their last night of a four-night workweek and the other on their first, so more officers filled the room than usual. Cracroft updated the patrol officers with the latest criminal highlights in the Watch Command Log folder.

0900 hours, suspicious death, 260 South West Temple

Passerby called when he observed a man down and bleeding in the parking lot located north of the Perry Hotel. Upon arrival, Officers Gruber and D. Findlay determined that this (approximately) 55-year-old white male had descended about 90 feet off the three-story hotel. Marks on the edge of the roof suggested this man did not want to fall. At the time of this writing, the M.E. is rolling fingerprints in hopes that an identification can be made. This man had a beard, medium-brown graying hair, and tattoos on both arms.

1149 hours, robbery, 877 West 800 South (Little Caesar's)

This was the second time this week that the establishment had been robbed by the same subject. The subject confronted the clerk, Ignacio Rodriguez, held his hand inside his jacket to intimate a gun and demanded money. The subject was unhappy with the small amount of money he received from the cash register and attempted to get behind the counter but found the door locked. He then fled westbound down Genesee Avenue. Subject described as male, white, 50s, 5'10", medium build, blond hair, mustache, possibly with a distinctively shaped nose, wearing a green windbreaker, green hat, and blue jeans.

1736 hours, child neglect/protective custody, 1684 Buccaneer Drive, Apt. B

Teresa B. Mansfield left her 6-month-old son, Steven, in her apartment alone. She contacted the downstairs neighbor and asked her to listen for the infant while she ran to the library for ten minutes. When officers arrived, the mother had been gone for about two hours. There was no electricity in the house. Detective Price and DCFS responded and took the child into protective custody.

Then the sergeant gave the floor to Serio, who patted JJ awake. They walked to the front of the room, one of them drowsy, the other petrified. He never hesitated to barge through the door of a known gang hideout or to chase down a resisting criminal bigger than himself, but Serio feared public speaking. Still one of the youngest officers in the room, he addressed the spot in front of his shoes, not making eye contact with anyone.

"This is JJ. He's a bloodhound and my personal dog." JJ stood at his side while Serio nervously twirled one of his big, soft-as-velvet ears. "I've been working on an opportunity to bring him in. Bloodhounds are used throughout the country in different agencies for tracking down people. They specialize in scent dis-crimination, where you give them an odor and they try to find the source of that odor."

Some patrol officers were smiling at the large, friendly dog in their squad room, while others rolled their eyes at what they surmised to be a feel-good project from the captain.

"He doesn't bite," Serio continued. "You don't have to worry about that."

Few admitted it outside their circle of trusted friends, but the department's German shepherds frightened a number of officers, particularly when the dogs were off leash. "They still scare me from time to time," said Terry Fritz, deputy chief of the K9 Squad. "That's their purpose. When you've got an armed suspect ready to fight, you send those dogs who will bite hard, scare the living doo-doo out of you, and hopefully force you to comply." The patrol dogs on the K9 Squad had exceptional training, but accidental bites did happen. Every once in a while, a patrol dog, still amped after being released to apprehend a felon, came back and popped an officer. One look at JJ allevi-ated any such fear.

"The worst thing you'll get with JJ might be a big goober of slobber," said Serio. "JJ will be with me in my patrol car. Anytime there's a crime and you don't know where the suspect is, give me a call, and I'll try to see if it's a bloodhound deal."

He figured he wouldn't get any direct requests for JJ, but that didn't matter. He could bring JJ to the scene anyway. Not long out of the lineup that first night with JJ on the job, a call came over the radio about a burglary that had just occurred at a dry cleaning business in the southeastern part of the city. Serio heard multiple officers call out that they were en route. Nervous as he could ever remember being, but knowing that he had only six months to prove whether JJ had a place at the table, he got on the radio.

"This is Charlie 123, I'm en route to that call. Please try to limit foot traffic and stay out of the crime scene until I get there with my bloodhound."

A rookie cop just told veteran officers to "stay out" until he got there with his *Beverly Hillbillies* dog that they had met for the first time two hours ago. The boy had balls of steel or brains of mush. Fortunately, Serio got to the scene soon after the first two officers arrived, so they didn't have to stay out for long.

The sliding glass door of the dry cleaner's was shattered, and the cash register inside lay open on the floor. Along with fragments of glass, coins had scattered all over the place. Any bills that might have been in the register had gone with the burglar. Serio's heart was thumping, but he tried to remain calm. "You ready to go to *work?*" he asked JJ almost in a whisper as he sat him down just outside the entrance to the dry cleaners. JJ didn't reply. Serio slipped the harness over JJ's head and secured the leather straps around his body. "You want to go to *work?*" Serio asked again, quiet as the first time. JJ tilted his head and looked at Serio but still held his silence. Serio took a deep breath and clipped the leash to the D-ring on the harness. At the sound of the click, JJ let out a booming bay, his pent-up excitement finally released.

In all of JJ's training, he always had a pristine scent article to start a track. The cash register seemed the best choice, but Serio worried about JJ cutting his paws on the glass. Instead, he kept JJ just outside the broken window and presented the whole store to JJ's nose. He swept his arm low like a backhanded racquetball shot in front of JJ's foreface, directing his nose toward the inside of the store and said, "Go find!"

JJ started searching. Nose down, he swiveled his head back and forth, back and forth, nostrils flaring. The two other officers stood watching. The bloodhound proceeded along the sidewalk at the front of the store and around the corner. Serio followed. They hit a thick fringe of grass along the sidewalk, and Serio thought, *Okay, that's a bonus.* For a scent dog the transition in odor level from a concrete sidewalk to grass is probably like suspecting that the kitchen trash can smells funky and then confirming, *Whew, that's nasty,* after opening the lid. JJ hooked into the track heading due east, pulling hard along the sidewalk. Serio looked ahead and saw Sergeant Cracroft walking due west right toward them. *Oh shit, he's messing up the track,* Serio thought. JJ was going to run right up to his patrol sergeant and start baying.

A minute earlier Cracroft had parked his car in back of the dry cleaner's. When he got out, he heard a loud howl from the front of the store and started walking that way. Next thing he saw was JJ running right at him with Serio in tow. The bloodhound came within a foot of him, swerved around, and continued running east along the sidewalk. JJ didn't even look up at Cracroft. Serio did but only for a moment. JJ turned another corner to the south, and Cracroft followed. When he caught up to them, JJ was turning around in circles, sniffing the ground along the street in a darkened area. The dog had lost the track. Serio took JJ farther up the street to see if he could reacquire a scent, but he didn't pick anything up.

When Cracroft first heard about Serio bringing his bloodhound on patrol, he didn't know what to think. Cracroft knew Serio was a hard worker, but he didn't know about bloodhounds beyond what he'd seen in the movies—packs of the dogs chasing escaped convicts through Southern swamps. After he saw JJ work that night, he quickly adjusted to reality.

"It was very plain to me," Cracroft said, "that JJ got a track, knew exactly where the guy went, and followed him right to where he parked his car and lost the scent. That's exactly where I would have parked my car if I were going to do a burglary at that place."

Cracroft also appreciated that JJ took not the least interest in him when tracking, going right around him and continuing up the road. "If it had been a German shepherd and I'm in the way," Cracroft said, "they're going after *me*."

They didn't capture anyone, but Serio felt good about JJ's first deployment. He focused, ignored distractions, and worked with purpose until he lost the scent. He also showed his patrol sergeant and a few fellow officers that, although he might look a little funny, he was no joke.

The K9 officers didn't laugh—but for a different reason. They didn't want JJ around, and they certainly didn't want Serio interfering with their calls. About a week after JJ started, Serio was driving his beat on the east side of the city. He was *10-8*, available to respond to any new calls. The triple beep on the radio from dispatch got his attention.

"All units, be advised: Home invasion robbery just occurred. Officers are requested to respond to 565 East Ramona Avenue. Complainant says suspect ran out the back door. Charlie 135 and 136, do you copy?"

Both patrol officers acknowledged that they were en route.

From the dispatch details Serio thought it sounded like a potential bloodhound situation. The incident had just occurred, the suspect was on foot and might live in the area or go to ground nearby. The patrol officers who arrived at the scene agreed. The two victims had been robbed at gunpoint and tied up with duct tape. The armed robber was last seen running north from the house. The patrol officers called dispatch and asked for Serio and his bloodhound.

"Charlie 123, I'm en route to that call with my bloodhound," Serio radioed from about five minutes away. He flipped on his lights and drove fast. But his excitement lasted only a minute.

"This is Kilo 858. *K9* has arrived on the home invasion robbery."

The officer had stressed the word "K9," and Serio could sense the hostility. He anxiously continued driving toward the scene.

The K9 officer arrived, ready to deploy his German shepherd.

"We've got Serio and JJ en route," one of the patrol officers said. "We think it would be a good opportunity for the bloodhound."

Not happy, the K9 officer left the scene.

When Serio arrived, the patrol officers weren't exactly sure what had happened. Serio had a feeling that it was going to come back to bite him, but he also had to sink or swim. Each chance to work his dog gave him one more opportunity to prove what they could do. JJ picked up a short track that led down the alley behind the house for half a block. The trail died out when it hit the road. The suspect likely got in a car and was long gone. Still, the experience proved useful. Just as pilots need to log long hours before getting their licenses, Serio and JJ had to keep on tracking before they could fly.

The fallout mixed hostility and frustration. The K9 officers didn't think Serio and his pet should have had the time of day. The K9 Squad handlers were the dog experts. They had years of field experience and scores of successful apprehensions to their credit. Their dog teams went through rigorous training and demonstrated mastery of a whole series of skills for certification before being deployed on the street. But out of the blue a rookie cop was chatting up the captain and telling the chief that his floppy-eared dog was what the K9 program needed? He'd gone to a training seminar in California and who knew where else, and just like that, his dog was the magic tool they'd been missing to catch more criminals? They didn't think so.

Lacking both pretense and a broad enough perception of human psychology, Serio couldn't understand the animosity. He had a new idea and a blind desire to help; that was it. He didn't know yet the great lengths to which the Salt Lake City K9 Squad had gone to rebuild its image over the last decade. Hard changes went into effect, and the culture of the K9 program had evolved radically. Before Serio waltzed in with his bloodhound, they had finally begun to outdistance the memory of bad press, lawsuits, and exile.

MOUTH

A scissors bite is preferred, level bite accepted.

May 1976

Billed as the largest ballroom in America when it began as the Coconut Grove in 1931, the Terrace Ballroom in Salt Lake City by the 1950s had become a must-stop for the biggest names in the music industry when touring the West. Within its walls people could sway to the soft baritone of Nat King Cole or kick up their poodle skirts and high-water pants to Les Brown and His Band of Renown. Martin Denny, Dave Brubeck, the Kingston Trio, and the Beach Boys added their own signature sounds to the musical annals of the Terrace Ballroom. By the end of the 1960s, however, the names on the marquee had changed to attract a different type of audience. Rock and roll charged in with a bang.

The Doors, Pink Floyd, the Grateful Dead, Deep Purple, and Led Zeppelin—if you wanted to catch them live in Salt Lake City, you went to the Terrace Ballroom. Sold-out shows made the management happy, but the performances also brought ticket holders with an increasing disregard for the law. More and more of the Terrace's revenues went to repairing property damaged by fans during concerts. Additional security and police officers had to be hired. It was no doubt a surprise, then, when one of the most notable clashes between concertgoers and police happened on a night featuring a Latin musician known as the God-father of New Mexico Music.

Al Hurricane and his band, who had played for such legends as Fats Domino, Marvin Gaye, and Chuck Berry, had come from New Mexico to perform for a private party at the Terrace Ballroom. The region's growing Hispanic community often hosted large gatherings and celebrations in rented halls such as the Terrace. About 3,000 people attended that night, and Al didn't disappoint. Others did, though. After the performance a large fight broke out in front of the venue, involving roughly 250 people.

Salt Lake City police and multiple K9 teams were called to control the crowd. The police stopped the fight, but when they ordered the crowd to disperse—allegedly with racial slurs—rocks and bottles came raining down on them. So they used their dogs. Several people were bitten by the police dogs, many assert "unnecessarily," including one police officer who described the German shepherds that night as "chain saws on leashes."

Complaints of racial prejudice and excessive force came quickly. The American Civil Liberties Union of Utah, which ordinarily didn't undertake police abuse litigation, provided legal defense for those arrested and injured by beatings and dog bites. A decade had passed since the height of the civil rights movement, but blistering images of fire hoses and snarling German shepherds set loose on protestors still remained fresh in the public mind. The Terrace Ballroom incident, involving predominately white police officers with German shepherds among a mostly Hispanic crowd, dominated the news for a time, but it didn't have much staying power.

Widely criticized for its haste in taking legal action against the police department and the city, the ACLU gradually pulled away their resources. Judith Wolbach, a cooperating attorney with the ACLU's Utah affiliate office, was the last public lawyer left standing. Overwhelmed and unable to support the legal efforts alone when the ACLU effectively dropped out, Wolbach couldn't continue. Private attorneys quietly resolved the cases.

Despite the legal misfire Wolbach maintains that the ACLU's involvement resulted in heightened sensitivity to ethnic issues in the region and the police department's future reluctance to use dogs in crowd control. Less than two years after the Terrace Ballroom incident, the Salt Lake City Police Department completely disbanded the K9 program. Although Police Chief

Officer Rose Cox trains her German shepherd patrol dog.
Photograph courtesy of Salt Lake City Police Department

Bud Willoughby cited budgetary reasons for the decision, many police officers directly attributed the end of the K9 program to the lawsuits stemming from the night when Al Hurricane came to town.

Salt Lake City had been using police dogs since 1959, the first city west of the Mississippi to do so, and ended the program in 1978. They weren't the only ones. Throughout the 1970s and '80s, other cities across the country concluded that the legal risks and image problems of their police dogs outweighed their advantages. It took the passing of twelve years and the tenacity of one woman to get dogs back on the beat in Salt Lake City.

• • •

Judy Dencker worked as a secretary for the Public Safety Commissioner for several years before switching jobs in the early '70s to become a dispatcher for the Salt Lake City Police Department. After two and a half years as "the voice on the other side of the radio," Dencker changed jobs again. Her new duties still required her to respond to emergency calls from the public—but no longer on the other end of the phone line. She had to show up in person instead. In 1973 Judy Dencker came aboard as a police officer. She and two other women became the first three female police officers to work on patrol in Salt Lake City.

As a rookie, proving yourself can be tough in the best of circumstances. Dencker and the other new female officers faced a greater challenge still. Many of the male officers had a hard time accepting them as equals, and some of the supervisors didn't want a woman working in their divisions. The extra attention from outside the department didn't help matters, either. As Dencker said, "The media were all over us like carp on corn."

In some cases it's fortunate that newness doesn't last long. The sight of female patrol officers became routine, and they proved themselves more than capable. As a young patrol officer, Dencker once had to wrest a gun away from a man who had shot himself in the head, but hadn't died, before paramedics could enter the apartment to treat him. Her kneecap broke during the arrest of another individual who didn't feel like being arrested. "While the job is exciting," Dencker acknowledged, "it does change your life." To unwind, she walked her dog.

From rookie patrol officer to sergeant, SWAT team commander, and captain of the Homicide Division, Dencker's thirty-year police career brims with accolades and high-profile leadership positions. However, many of Salt Lake's police K9 handlers remember her best as a lieutenant in 1989.

Earlier in her career, working the graveyard shift on the city's west side, Dencker often responded to calls of alarms going off in large warehouses and industrial buildings. One or two officers couldn't search the entire building and contain the outside. Dencker had to call the Salt Lake County Sheriff's Office. "Hey, can you send one of your dogs over?" While Chief Willoughby had bowed to pressure and disbanded Salt Lake City's K9 program, Sheriff Pete Hayward took a damn-the-torpedoes approach and kept the sheriff's German shepherds working as usual.

"Aside from the fact that it was kind of embarrassing not having dogs of our own," Dencker said, "I got tired of calling the sheriff's office every time." They often arrived too late. She researched how police dogs were being trained and discovered to her surprise that training had taken a 180-degree turn from the bite-and-chew approach that had landed so many K9 programs in trouble. With a German shepherd of her own named Rocky, Dencker started hanging out with the K9 handlers from the sheriff's office and the West Valley Police Department to learn the aspects of training firsthand and to see the dogs' full range of capabilities.

Much like Serio did some sixteen years later, she put a dog proposal together. More experienced and higher up the chain, Dencker arranged a meeting directly with the chief to present her plan. But less than two minutes into her presentation, Willoughby heard the word "dogs" and ended the meeting. "We're not going to have dogs," he said. "No way in hell."

Dencker went back to calling the sheriff's office whenever they needed dogs on the graveyard shift and continued training with the other K9 handlers in the valley. After a few years, she tried Willoughby again.

"Don't ever bring this up to me again," he said flatly.

She didn't, but she had the advantage of youth. Willoughby retired in 1988.

At a social gathering with Salt Lake City's new chief, Mike Chabries, Dencker asked, "So what do you think about dogs?"

"What are we waiting for?" Chabries asked after she made a more formal presentation a week later.

The K9 Squad was reborn. They secured funding for four German shepherds—imported from Germany—one K9 sergeant, three K9 officers, and three Chevy S-10 Blazers specially equipped for police dogs. Officers in other units complained about the expensive new wheels, but Dencker cited the importance of getting dogs to the scene, no matter the weather or road conditions. "What's the point of having a railway locomotive if you don't have tracks?"

Police officials asked Dencker if the K9 Squad could use her German shepherd, Rocky. He was already trained, would be a solid addition to the team (and cynically, he wouldn't cost the department any more money). Dencker was already in the process of being promoted to lieutenant, so she said, "Sure, if I can be the lieutenant over K9." New appointments didn't work like that, however, and the administration said no. "Well, then," Dencker responded, "I'm going to take my ball and go home." Assigned elsewhere, she remained a strong voice of support for the K9 program, and Rocky remained a beloved pet.

Press releases carefully stated that the new German shepherd police dogs wouldn't be used for crowd control. "You could even have your kids come eat marshmallows with our dogs," Dencker said, "and they won't bite." Training dogs to be alligators on leashes belonged to the past. They emphasized a totally different type of training: teaching dogs to find evidence, search buildings, apprehend uncooperative suspects, and protect officers. Not much press surrounded Salt Lake's new K9 program, but the little they got was all positive.

For the police positive press is good, but no press at all is sometimes better. Dencker knew that many people would be examining the rebooted K9 program under a microscope. Walking on eggshells, Sergeant Don Campbell and K9 officers Marty Kaufman, Mark Nelson, and Jon Richey took the kindest and gentlest approach they could with dogs trained to chase, bite, and hold onto a limb with forty-two sharp teeth that could deliver four hundred pounds of pressure per square inch.

Over nearly a decade, the Salt Lake City K9 Squad had built a solid reputation with hard work, dedication, community outreach, and, fortunately, little press coverage. They had risen from disbandment to become one of the premier K9 squads in the country, with handlers and dogs consistently winning top honors at police K9 competitions throughout the West. In that context it's easy to imagine why they reluctantly embraced or even acknowledged a rookie cop coming from outside the ranks with an entirely new kind of dog. Serio couldn't see this at the time, however.

He still had to cover his regular patrol beat as usual, so many nights he had no interaction with the K9 officers. On nights when their paths did cross, though, he got the cold shoulder. So he decided to focus on showing JJ in action to as many fellow patrol officers as possible. Sergeant Cracroft's acceptance offered a big nod of approval, but word of mouth travels only so far. Serio knew that for skeptical officers exposed to many tall tales only seeing is believing.

On a typical call while working patrol, such as a domestic violence incident or dealing with the drunk and disorderly—by no means mutually exclusive—Serio exited the car and left the windows cracked open, and JJ slept on the rear bench seat. After his responsibilities on the call ended, Serio got one of the other patrol officers at the scene to help him train his dog.

"We'd take off for a few blocks and hide, getting a fifteen- to thirty-minute head start," said police detective Robin Snyder, one of the many uniformed volunteers whom Serio enlisted. "JJ would always find us."

Even if the track was short and easy, Serio wanted to get his dog out and show the other officers what he could do. When they had a little more time on a slow night, Serio recruited the help of two officers, one to lay the track and the other to follow him and JJ. Serio sometimes set up known tracks, where he knew the officer had gone, so he could explain to the officer behind him what JJ was doing along the way. More often, however, he used unknown tracks, where he had no idea in which direction the officer had gone, letting JJ speak for himself. Once the officers witnessed JJ at work, the connection clicked. They saw right away just how applicable the bloodhound could be in scenarios they routinely encountered on the job.

Two weeks into his police career, JJ was making a solid impression on the patrol officers who had seen him train, but other than his first night, he wasn't getting many chances to work on actual calls. At 3:40 a.m. on October 2, 1999, dispatch reported a vandalism that occurred at 1859 East Logan Avenue, a house in a high-income neighborhood on the east side of town. The K9 Squad wouldn't respond to such a call. Obnoxious as vandals are, police dogs aren't allowed to bite them because they're not felons. Serio and JJ got the all clear.

They arrived at the scene as quickly as possible. A large ceramic planter had gone through the victim's bay window. Given the size, Serio figured that it had taken more than one person to throw it. Glass, planter shards, and flowers lay scattered on the front lawn and throughout the house. All Serio could smell was the earthy aroma of rich potting soil. He was hoping his bloodhound could smell more.

Serio scented JJ off the planter shards on the front lawn. Nose down, he detailed the ground, circled the front yard, and started west along the north side of the street. Officer Jeff Kolva followed on foot. Working the trail aggressively, JJ pulled Serio for a quarter of a mile along the sidewalk, passing more than twenty houses, then turned north on Bryan Avenue. He approached the house at 1705 East Bryan Avenue, and they discovered another broken planter pot smashed against the front wall. Serio called it in over the radio, and JJ continued north, then east toward Clayton Middle School. As JJ pulled Serio onto the school grounds and headed toward the playground in back, dispatch called out another vandalism of the same nature at 2246 East Roosevelt Avenue, about half a mile farther east of their location.

Officer Kolva ran back to get his patrol car and gave Serio and JJ a ride to the latest sighting. Serio knew that JJ was working a fresh scent and wanted to jump ahead to have a chance at catching the vandals. Arriving at the new house, he scented JJ off another broken pot, and they were on the move again. JJ tracked for two and half miles, passing more vandalized houses along the way, before he lost the scent in a crowded neighborhood. Serio guessed that the suspects lived somewhere in the vicinity or got into a car nearby.

Officer Kolva and the other patrol officers out that night didn't need to read the minutia of JJ's body language to see that he was hot on the trail. The string of vandalized houses to which JJ brought them was evidence enough, and they later learned that the back side of Clayton Middle School, where JJ was headed before they hopped in the car to the next house, had been vandalized in the same manner.

Serio took pride in his dog—but they hadn't caught anyone. Many accounts of police bloodhounds tell remarkable tales of a dog trailing long distances over difficult terrain, hours or even days after the crime has occurred. The story usually winds down with the dog losing the scent or being pulled from the trail because of exhaustion. But that's usually not the end of the story. Apprehended days or weeks later by other police officers and questioned about his path, the criminal confirms that he traveled the same path that the bloodhound followed. Such accounts offer impressive examples of a bloodhound's skills, but according to the Salt Lake City Police Department's standards, they would still be logged officially as unsuccessful deployments.

Serio didn't want to be a fisherman with great tales of the ones that got away. A week later, he got another chance to cast his dog.

NOSTRILS

The nostrils are large and open.

October 1999

The triple beep got everyone's attention. "All units, be advised: Carjacking just occurred. Suspect vehicle crashed into car at intersection of 2300 East and Parleys Way. Female victim injured at the scene reports carjacking suspect fled on foot."

Serio arrived at the scene within a few minutes. The front end of a 1984 silver Nissan Maxima was wrapped in a violent embrace around the right rear bumper of a brand new black Jeep Cherokee. Officer Cody Lougy stood by the crash trying to gather information from a young woman crying and talking non-stop. A hitchhiker had taken her car with her in it, drove erratically, crashed, and ran off. Witnesses at the scene confirmed the last part; they had seen a tall white male, medium build, exit the car and run south.

Serio got JJ out and harnessed him up. Despite having a witness-confirmed direction, the start of the scent trail was going to be difficult. The crash had occurred near a busy intersection where two main roads met in a V and merged to form a larger road. Although it was 1:15 in the morning, traffic continued to pass by. Serio introduced JJ to the driver's seat of the silver Nissan Maxima, commanded "Go find!" and started casting his dog on the outer edges of the busy intersection. Officer Jeff Bedard followed, his first time behind a bloodhound. JJ picked up a track on the pavement and headed southwest through the empty parking lot of a Papa Murphy's Take 'n' Bake and behind a Phillips 66 gas station.

Serio worried a little that JJ wasn't baying, but he felt confident that, nostrils flaring and working like a Hoover upright across the asphalt, JJ was on to something. When they reached the corner of the next street, JJ let out a short bay and pulled south on Dallin Street. That's what Serio had been hoping for . . . until a hundred yards farther down the street JJ veered off the sidewalk to circle a large pine tree, his tail wagging. In the nearly pitch-black night, Serio and Bedard shone their flashlights on the tree. Green and healthy, thick branches bisected the tree trunk from top to bottom, creating a wide skirt where it met the ground.

This was only JJ's third time tracking someone he didn't know, and the dog's intensity didn't reach the level Serio thought it should. He wasn't baying or pulling hard, just slowly sniffing and circling. With the neighborhood so near the mouth of a canyon where the Wasatch Mountains leveled off to the city, there was also a good chance that a large four-legged creature resided in the tree.

"*Jay*, don't be tracking raccoons," Serio said to his dog. The officers' flashlights didn't reveal anything beyond branches bursting with pine needles. Serio pulled JJ away from the tree, hoping that after the distraction they could reacquire the scent trail. JJ pulled back and wouldn't leave. He kept circling the tree, growing more intent.

"Jeff," Serio said to Bedard, "I think we really need to get in this pine tree. Pull these branches back, and see what we're missing here."

As Serio and Bedard started lifting the heavy branches at the base of the tree, JJ started his rolling bay. He wanted to get under there. Then Bedard grabbed an ankle, yanked hard, and dragged a man into the beam of his flashlight. Twenty-six years old, 170 pounds, and six feet tall—had he not been sprawled across the ground—the man didn't resist. He was drunk and apologetic. "I fucked up, I'm sorry. I'll pay for the damages." Bedard slapped on the handcuffs.

"*Good boy,*" Serio praised JJ, vigorously rubbing his sides and petting his head. Strips of beef jerky appeared, to the dog's delight. The bloodhound had made his first criminal find: a kidnapping carjacker. A few hours later, before the end of their shift, Serio learned that the man had been charged with a DUI and a hit and run. The injured woman, taken to the hospital after complaints of a sore neck and back, was also being charged. She had lied to the police. The man was her boyfriend, a waiter at T.G.I. Friday's. She had made up the carjacking story so he could get away. The lowered severity of the crime dampened Serio's enthusiasm, but not for long. JJ had still chalked up his first apprehension in under a month on the job.

One bad guy down, countless more to go.

• • •

Winning the support of the patrol officers was critical. They are the first responders to the majority of crime scenes. They make the initial assessment and call in additional resources as necessary. A patrol officer with his own designated beat, Serio could only work JJ when he was free or specifically requested. As more and more of the other patrol officers saw JJ at work, deployment opportunities increased. It also helped that Serio wasn't picky. He deployed his dog on all manner of calls. As long as there was a chance the suspect left on foot and the police didn't know where to find him, Serio got JJ out and started looking.

Some of the K9 officers criticized Serio, saying he was too quick to deploy his dog on petty crimes. Years later Serio would probably agree with the criticism, but as a young officer with a short trial period to show what a bloodhound could do, he didn't care.

"I don't care if they're garden gnome thieves," Serio said. "I just want to get my dog on the track."

While they never caught a gnome thief, Serio and JJ hauled in others. Two weeks after JJ's first apprehension, they were called to help search for a domestic assault suspect who had fled just before police arrived. The victim said the suspect ran behind the house and east through an alley. When Serio and JJ got there, other officers had already been searching the block for about 25 minutes with no luck. JJ picked up a strong scent in the alley behind the house and led Serio to a neighbor's garage two houses away. Serio opened the garage door and saw a truck but no one inside. JJ insistently sniffed the truck's door handle. Hiding in the footwell below the rear bench seat was JJ's second criminal find.

Later that same month JJ was sniffing a pair of underwear—not recreationally, as he often did—but as part of the job. Ronald Chavez had beaten his wife and fled the house on foot a few minutes before the police showed up. When Serio asked the victim for a recently worn article of Ronald's clothing, she gave him the underwear. JJ smelled it, bayed, and took off to the backyard. He circled around to the side yard and sniffed the closed lids of two large trash cans. The victim had said that her husband likely would have gone to the park, so Serio thought JJ was smelling food that he wanted in the trash. He pulled him away to pick up an outer trail leading away from the house. JJ refused to leave the area, though, and brought Serio back to the trash cans. Circling, jumping up, and putting his paws on the cans, JJ finally zeroed in on the one on the right and poked his nostrils at the lid. Serio found Chavez buried in trash inside it, smelling awful. He was arrested for domestic battery.

Arriving home each morning after his graveyard shift, Serio tried to be quiet so he wouldn't wake up Lisa. JJ wasn't always as considerate. Lisa didn't have to ask Serio what kind of night they'd had. JJ told her. If he caught someone, he headed straight for the bedroom, jumped on the bed, and nudged her awake. "He had an awareness of what he was doing," Lisa said. "I don't know how that's possible, but he knew he did something good and was really proud of it." After nights when he didn't have a find, JJ let her sleep.

Perhaps wanting to end the millennium on a clean note, December 1999 made for a slow month for crimes befitting a bloodhound. Lisa got to sleep in for a while. When the sky didn't fall on New Year's Eve of Y2K, the criminals of Salt Lake City started 2000 like any other year: with lots of activity. On January 1 JJ recorded his first double capture, nabbing two suspects in separate incidents on the same night. The first came in response to a witness who called saying that she had seen two juveniles firing a handgun into the air near her house. Serio scented JJ off footprints in the snow, and JJ tracked between houses, through a field, across a creek, into another neighborhood, and directly to a trailer home.

Hearing loud, strange howls, one of the suspects, completely unaware he was being tracked, poked his head out the back door to see what was going on and why his pit bull terrier, tied to a post in the front yard, was whining, scared, and pulling on his rope to get away. Once the suspect saw a big bloodhound leashed to a police officer coming his way, he slammed the door shut. More units were called in to surround the home. The police entered, located the suspects and a .380 pistol, and took the sixteen-year-old shooter, a restricted person with a previous felony offense, to the juvenile detention center.

Later that night it was snowing heavily as JJ followed the trail of a burglary suspect a few blocks southeast of downtown Salt

Lake. Footprints appeared in some places, but an inch of snow covered the freshest prints, not always easy to discern from the many others still on the ground. JJ's nose knew just which ones to follow, though, and Serio trusted him.

Good fences may make good neighbors, but they also make following a scent trail with a bloodhound an arduous process. Serio guessed that the suspect was a career burglar who knew he might be followed because the trail seemed deliberately difficult. They had to "jump" (i.e., lift bloodhound and heave) fence after fence through multiple neighborhood blocks. For stretches of the trail with only fresh powder, Serio figured the suspect had walked along the top of the fences to avoid disturbing the snow. JJ finally stopped outside a small brick house nearly a mile from the crime scene. He walked around to the back, then to the front and back again, over and over. JJ couldn't find an outer scent trail from the house, and Serio saw no footprints in the snow leading away. The bloodhound began to focus on the garage in back, nearly as big as the house itself. Serio and Officer Kari Sanders opened the garage and noticed wet footprints inside leading to a large shed. JJ sniffed and scratched at the bottom of the shed door.

Once a suspect is assumed to be in an enclosed area, the job of a nonbiting dog is done. German shepherds in particular excel in this type of situation. The officers could yell their own version of *olly olly in come free*, adding, "If you don't, we're sending in the dog." Without a biting dog around, however, it's up to the well-armed officers to extract the uncooperative suspect.

Not wanting to subject JJ to potential injury from a cornered suspect, Serio tied his leash outside. He and Sanders entered the shed. Packed from floor to ceiling with old tools, lawn equipment, gas cans, and boxes, the shed was hard to navigate. After a quick but relatively thorough search, they couldn't locate anyone. Serio got JJ again and let him search the shed to see if they might have missed anything. The dog padded his way through the clutter, flipped his nose beneath a green tarp on a lower shelf in the back corner, and wagged his tail rapidly. Thinking a human couldn't possibly be back there, Serio guessed that JJ had found a cat. He lifted the tarp and saw a black leather jacket and a head of hair. When Serio grabbed the man, he started fighting, JJ bayed, and Sanders rushed over to help put him in handcuffs. The suspect was booked for burglary, possession of methamphetamines, and an aggravated assault warrant. JJ got lots of praise and a Milk-Bone.

Before January ended JJ had tracked down a loaded shotgun and handgun used by a gang in a drive-by shooting and, in a separate incident, found a seventeen-year-old boy that the Salt Lake County sheriff's department had been pursuing at high speed before he wrecked a stolen vehicle and fled on foot. Jumping three fences and locating a discarded sweatshirt in a basement laundry room, Serio and JJ eventually found the boy as he was pretending to knock on the door of someone's house shortly before 8:00 a.m.

"It was a nonchalant kind of thing," said Deputy John Taylor, who was with Serio and JJ that night. "He wanted to be depicted as a regular citizen, but he couldn't fool that dog." The *Deseret News,* Utah's oldest daily newspaper, wrote an article about the car chase and the bloodhound that found the teenage thief. It was JJ's first news coverage. Word was out: JJ was destined to be a media hound.

Four days later NBC's Utah affiliate, Channel 5 KSL News, got in on the action. Serio and JJ were enjoying a well-earned day off when Sergeant Jed Hurst called and asked if they'd come in

The media hound hams it up for the local news.
*Photograph courtesy of Mark DiOrio/*Deseret News

and help look for a burglary suspect who had eluded officers. It was the first time Serio had been asked to bring JJ when not on duty. He arrived at the scene around 2:00 p.m. wearing jeans and a ski jacket because he didn't want to lose time changing into uniform. Even though the temperature was hovering around twenty-eight degrees Fahrenheit, he felt more nervous than cold. A ton of police officers were milling around, and a search party, including a K9 team with a German shepherd, had already been looking for the suspect.

Two and a half hours had passed since the police lost sight of the burglar near Liberty Park, a few blocks south of downtown. Fortunately, the suspect had dropped his backpack while running from the police. It contained a sweatshirt, so JJ had a good scent article and a last known location. A few blocks away the trail led to that most dreaded of apparel items in Boston and Baltimore: a Yankees baseball cap. Wet with sweat, the blue hat lay behind a trash can in an alley between two houses. JJ lunged, trying to get to it. He reacquired the trail and took Serio up the steps to the back door of a house farther up the block. Officer Bruce Evans and Serio knocked on the door.

A tall young man named Kasey Keenan answered. Except for his clothes, he fit the general description of the suspect and appeared anxious. Not wagging his tail at all, JJ sniffed him heavily but didn't identify him by sitting and baying. JJ usually wagged his tail when meeting someone new unless the person was scared and emitting an adrenaline scent. Also, Kasey had just come from the shower. His hair was wet, and he was cleanly shaven. Serio thought he still might be their guy. The freshly washed smell may have confused JJ.

"Do you own a Yankees baseball cap?" Serio asked.

"No, I don't," Kasey replied.

The officers hadn't seen the suspect enter the house, so they couldn't go in without a warrant. They were free to look around outside, however, and that's where Sergeant Hurst and Serio found a handful of burned Polaroid photographs on the ground in the backyard, just outside the window. Most of the photos were damaged beyond recognition—but one wasn't. It was a good picture of Kasey, tall, handsome, smiling. He was wearing a blue Yankees baseball cap. When the officers showed him the photograph, he turned his head with shame and later confessed to the burglary after more evidence surfaced and the victim identified him.

"You could call him the Salt Lake City Police Department's secret weapon," said Keith McCord, the mustached KSL News anchorman with a sonorous voice. "A new breed of officer with a track record of always getting his man."

"JJ the bloodhound has been on the force just five months now," continued coanchor Carole Mikita with perfect timing and elocution, "but already he's sniffed out eleven bad guys."

"Not bad," said McCord. "News specialist Jill Atwood has more."

A clip followed of Serio, holding a plastic sandwich bag in front of JJ's nose, as he demonstrated the start of a track. "You ready to go to *work*?"

JJ jumped and bayed, his howl picked up perfectly by the news cameraman's microphone.

"Meet JJ, Salt Lake City's newest crime fighter," a voiceover by Jill Atwood began as the scenes alternated between Lisa walking away fast, laying a track, and JJ sniffing the ground and lunging forward. "Give him a scent and he'll sniff it out, usually leading police straight to the bad guys."

Interview responses of Serio followed, talking about when he first observed JJ's unique tracking skills as a puppy. The segment then featured the burglary case and showed scenes of Kasey Keenan being put into a patrol car in handcuffs.

"I think this bloodhound has a future in this department," said Sergeant Hurst. "He's been doing a really good job for us."

"That's why he's good at what he does," Serio said before the scene cut to JJ rounding a tree to find Lisa, his whole body wagging as he sat at her feet to indicate the end of the trail. "He likes people. He likes to find what he's looking for. So that's his reward."

"Now, unlike German shepherds in the K9 unit," anchorwoman Mikita said, back in the newsroom, winding down the segment but stirring up the tension with the K9 Squad, "JJ is not aggressive, doesn't have that killer instinct, so he's perfect for sniffing out misdemeanor cases, even missing children cases."

"Give that dog a badge," said McCord before segueing into a story about uninsured drivers in Utah.

Serio thrilled at seeing his dog on television, and the police administration certainly liked the positive coverage. The timing couldn't have been better, either. It came at the tail end of the six-month trial period. Now Serio needed to put together a summary report of their work and a plan for going forward. Further adding to the good timing, the K9 Squad had recently put out a request for applications because of the expected turnover of some of their handlers. Serio decided to combine the report and application into one document. On the "Position Applied For" line, he wrote: "Requesting Bloodhound Program become an addition to our current K9 Program."

The response that Serio got wasn't at all what he expected. After the patrol lineup at the start of his shift one night, K9 Sergeant Don Campbell told Serio to meet him in his office. Campbell had supported the bloodhound program early, and even though some of the K9 handlers on his squad hadn't been so welcoming, Serio appreciated the role that Campbell had played in getting approval for the trial period.

Serio sat down, JJ lay on the floor, and Campbell shut the door. Right away Serio knew something was wrong.

"I just wanted to let you know that I appreciate all your hard work," said Campbell. "You've done a decent job with JJ, but it's not working out like I expected or the department had hoped. From here on out, the trial period is over. You're not supposed to bring JJ to work anymore."

"I don't understand," Serio said, looking down at JJ, who if he'd been paying attention wouldn't have understood either. "Everything is going so well. I've got a lot of support. I'm catching a lot of bad guys and still working patrol." His confusion quickly turned to anger. "I'm keeping par with the other K9 handlers, probably even significantly more than they've been doing, as far as apprehensions go."

That last comment tellingly brought Campbell to a shared state of anger. He didn't like the comparison to his K9 Squad. But the numbers were hard to argue against. In fewer than six months, Serio and JJ had twelve criminal finds resulting in ten arrests, eleven trails leading to evidence, and four trails that produced valuable leads. All this while still managing his patrol duties. The statistics matched the top German shepherd handler and exceeded others.

Following more tense words and additional requests from Serio for an explanation that made sense, the conclusion remained the same: "After tonight don't bring JJ to work with you anymore," Campbell repeated.

Except for calling Lisa, Serio didn't talk to anybody that night about what had happened. Feeling sick at heart, he completed his last night with JJ in a daze of hurt and outrage.

• • •

Despite what the Utah Heritage Foundation believes, the Public Safety Building that houses the Liberty Police Station on the east side of Salt Lake City is one of the ugliest buildings in the city: eight stories of soap scum–colored glass, stone, and steel that looks more like a rhombus than a rectangle. As Serio left by the back door of the station that morning heading home, he spotted Captain Scott Folsom, who oversaw the K9 Squad, among many other duties. Until that night Serio had counted him as one of his strongest supporters in the administration.

"Hello, Mike," Captain Folsom said, starting his day. Tired and understandably dejected at the end of his shift, Serio mumbled a greeting. Folsom asked him how it was going, clearly seeing that it hadn't been a great night for the officer.

"I apologize for asking you this right here and now," said Serio. "I was just wondering what went wrong with the bloodhound program and why it was terminated."

"What?" Folsom responded. "I haven't given authorization for anyone to do that."

Serio explained what Campbell had told him.

"No one discussed it with me," Folsom reiterated, stiffening. "Just stand by. I'll call you by the afternoon."

Serio went home, not sure what to think.

Later that afternoon, as promised, Folsom called. "Continue bringing JJ to work. Wait for further details."

Even though spring was approaching, the temperature dropped a few degrees anytime Serio and Campbell neared each other. They never again discussed the conversation in Campbell's office. All further communications about Serio's role with JJ came from Lieutenant Kyle Jones, Campbell's immediate

Serio puts JJ's harness on as JJ bays, ready to work.
*Photograph courtesy of Mark DiOrio/*Deseret News

supervisor . . . until late April. Then Serio had to communicate with Campbell on a daily basis. A new *Agreement for Use of a Bloodhound* was drawn up.

Gone was the "experimental program to determine whether or not a bloodhound would be of use to police operations." Other changes to the K9 agreement held that the city now would pay for all of JJ's food and routine veterinary expenses. His value, should he be killed in the line of duty, increased from five hundred to a thousand dollars. A new six-month trial period went into effect—but this time with Serio and JJ as official members of the K9 Squad.

Still the unwelcome stepchild, at least JJ the bloodhound was now part of the family.

PART TWO

HEROES AND GOATS

A hound it was, an enormous coal-black hound, but
not such a hound as mortal eyes have ever seen.
Fire burst from its open mouth, its eyes glowed with
a smouldering glare, its muzzle and hackles and
dewlap were outlined in flickering flame.

—**Sir Arthur Conan Doyle,**
The Hound of the Baskervilles

LIPS, FLEWS, AND DEWLAP

In front the lips fall squarely, making a right angle with the upper line of the foreface; whilst behind they form deep, hanging flews, and, being continued into the pendant folds of loose skin about the neck, constitute the dewlap, which is very pronounced.

January 2001

Troy Fuller—white male, late thirties, five foot ten, 190 pounds, green eyes, red Toyota pickup—was leading a high-risk life with a low probability of reaching old age. A jack of most illegal trades, he had sixty-one criminal charges to his credit. Larceny, aggravated burglary, felony fleeing, resisting arrest, drug possessions of every sort, and multiple DUIs comprised just a few of the highlights.

A full week after New Year's Eve, Troy Fuller was still celebrating. Around midnight he was driving with a license revoked for a previous alcohol offense. In a residential neighborhood on the west side of the city, his vehicle veered off to the left, jumped the curb, grazed a tree, took out two separate mailboxes, and came to an abrupt stop with the help of a parked 1993 blue Chevy Cavalier. Troy could defy all the laws of the state of Utah, but he couldn't thwart the laws of physics—Newton's first law of motion to be precise: An object in motion tends to remain in motion unless an external force acts against it.

Inside the truck Troy's head was the object in motion, and the now stationary steering wheel became the external force applied against it. His face lost at the meeting point. The steering wheel lacerated his lower lip so severely it almost completely detached it from his mouth. A neighbor came out and saw Troy emerge from the vehicle. "It's not my car," he managed to say. "I gotta go." And off he went.

It wasn't his car, but he shouldn't have left—and not just because leaving the scene added a hit-and-run charge to his tally. He was drunk, injured, more than fifteen miles from home, and on foot in weather ten degrees below freezing.

Serio arrived at the scene first and scented JJ off blood on the ground near the truck. It's not often that a bloodhound scents off actual blood, but it's a good start. JJ went north for about fifty yards, then took a sharp left toward the back of a house. Serio didn't have any additional witnesses to indicate where the suspect had fled, and no visible evidence—drops of blood, an open gate, footprints in the moist grass or pockets of snow— demonstrated that he had gone behind the house. Serio didn't think it a natural choice for the suspect to flee in that direction, so he pulled JJ off the track and encouraged him to continue north toward a main cross street another six houses up the road.

JJ obliged, but at the cross street he went left for the width of the house on the corner and turned left again, bringing Serio behind the row of houses they had just passed. Once JJ got behind the backyard fence of the same house he had first indicated, he let out his signature bay and pulled hard to the right. Serio kicked himself for not trusting his dog. Fears of following JJ on a long track that led to a particularly good-smelling cat still preyed on his mind.

JJ tracked through more backyards, over fences, across a street, and into a new subdivision. JJ turned south and brought Serio through a few more backyards before finally locating a man behind a house, face down in the snow. The man had passed out, not responding to any verbal challenges. Serio could see that he was bleeding badly.

The fire department's medical personnel arrived and managed to get Troy sitting up in the back of the ambulance where they could assess his injuries. Serio was free to go at that point. K9 officers rarely make arrests. For the German and Belgian shepherd handlers, the concern is that their dogs might eat an arrestee before getting back to the station. For Serio the concern was that JJ would lovingly slobber all over a criminal who didn't deserve it.

Officer Jason Miller, a young patrolman widely regarded as one of the best beat cops in the department, arrived to read Troy his Miranda rights, letting him know, if it wasn't already clear, that he was under arrest. The medics said that, given the temperature and Troy's condition, he would have frozen to death had JJ and Serio not found him. Officer Miller followed the ambulance to the hospital and accompanied Troy, still reeking of alcohol, to be treated for his injuries.

"Were you driving the car?" a nurse asked Troy as she checked his vitals.

"Last I remember, I *think* I was driving." Troy touched the bandage that kept his lower lip in place. "I think I ate my steering wheel. It didn't taste too good. Am I going to live through this?"

"Yes," the nurse replied.

"Good. If not, I'm gonna kill myself. I don't believe I hit a parked car. Shoot me."

When the blood technician arrived to draw his blood, Troy asked him, "Are you God?"

"No," replied the phlebotomist.

"You're Lucifer. Lucifer is here. I know I did something wrong now."

● ● ●

JJ's charm worked wonders on the other patrol officers, dispatchers—who loved to hear his bay over the radio—and the community in general. His magnetism hadn't won him any fans with the other K9 handlers, however, nor with the growing number of captured criminals he kept adding to his tally. The media stories about "the police bloodhound who always gets his man" may have caused some resentment from the German shepherd handlers, but what really burned was that patrol officers began requesting JJ by name. Campbell had moved to another position, after serving as Serio's K9 sergeant for only three months. Sergeant C. T. Smith took his place, which, along with the influx of three new K9 officers, helped dissipate some of the tension. Enough remained, however, to spark animosity anew whenever JJ got a curtain call for his services.

Since the tail end of their first trial period, JJ and Serio had been training nearly once a week with the Wasatch Front Multi-Agency K9 Association, a grouping of all the police K9 squads from the smaller agencies in the Salt Lake Valley. The Salt Lake City Police Department and the Salt Lake County Sheriff's Department were large enough to have full-time K9 units with multiple dogs on duty. The smaller agencies couldn't afford to do that, though, and on any given shift they often had only one dog to respond to calls or none at all. The multiagency group ensured that dispatch could call all participating departments when a K9 was requested, and dogs would come running, so to speak.

Glenn Smith, an officer from South Salt Lake, introduced Serio to Multi-Agency K9. As often happens in their world, Serio and Smith first met by way of a criminal. On a cold night in January 2000, Multi-Agency K9 officers were dispatched on a vehicle theft in which the suspect had crashed into a tree at the Nibley Park Golf Course and fled. Smith deployed his German shepherd, Erik, and tried to pick up a track leading away from the crashed vehicle. A Salt Lake City officer at the scene saw Smith working his dog without getting a solid lead and said, "Hey, we've got a bloodhound. Want me to call him over?"

A bloodhound? Smith knew that police on the East Coast used bloodhounds, but he had never heard of one in Utah. "Sure," he said, dubious but intrigued, "call him over."

Smith put his dog away and ran behind them for what seemed like miles. He had a hard time keeping up, not because he was out of shape but because a big strong dog can always pull you faster than you can run by yourself. They didn't catch the guy, but Smith was impressed. He had seen patrol dogs that were good trackers but nothing like JJ in terms of drive and distance. That night Smith invited Serio to train with the Multi-Agency K9 crew. They liked the new ideas that Serio brought to the group, and it helped their patrol dogs become better trackers. Serio learned new training methods, but he really valued the opportunity to work with a group of K9 officers who wanted him around.

Regular contact with other agencies helped spread the word of a new dog in town. Sergeant Brad Marshal worked for the Utah Highway Patrol. A friend in another agency had told him, "If you want to find somebody, call for JJ." When Marshal showed up at a scene where a stolen vehicle had rolled over in a highway pursuit and the occupants fled, he called Salt Lake City dispatch and asked for JJ. Marshal had never heard of Serio.

"Is that Officer JJ?" the dispatcher asked.

"Uh, I don't know," said Marshal. "I think that's the dog's name."

Serio pulled up in his K9 truck.

"I was thinking a bloodhound would be a smaller animal and was really surprised to see the small horse that came out of the vehicle," Marshal said later. "I was thinking maybe he was going to get a saddle for him."

Marshal followed as JJ tracked alongside heavy traffic, down an on-ramp, across the freeway, through a construction site, and over fences. Farther down the road he turned the corner and ran right up to a man using the pay phone at a convenience store.

With Serio holding him back, JJ reared up on his hind legs and bayed right in the man's face. "Apparently," said Marshal, "that's the dude." An eyewitness account and evidence soon showed that, indeed, that was the dude.

The dog had made an impression. When Marshal moved to a task force position tracking narcotics fugitives, he called on JJ some more. Whether it was the conditions of the cases or just good luck, JJ seemed to have a perfect track record when Marshal was on the scene. They always found their guy. A short time later Marshal indirectly learned that he couldn't call for JJ anymore; he had to call for a K9. "I guess some of the other K9 handlers' feelings were getting hurt." It wasn't personal for Marshal; he just wanted to catch the fugitive. After a few instances in which other dogs didn't find anybody for him, he got Serio's cell phone number so he could be a little more discreet.

Serio always showed up when requested, but he was also doing his best to fit in with his own K9 Squad and keep his nose clean. His role with JJ still felt tenuous, and he didn't want to give anyone easy access to anything easily used against him. But it was hard keeping everything balanced. On one of his days off, the West Valley Police Department called Serio to help look for an armed robbery suspect who had held up a convenience store at gunpoint. Serio had built a good relationship with the other K9 squads in the valley, and as the only police bloodhound team in Utah, they were getting more outside agency requests. Both his own department and other agencies had called him at home a few times before, and he always responded the same way: He got JJ, and off they went. What he didn't do was call his department and ask for approval to go.

I'm a police officer, and JJ's my dog, Serio thought—if he thought about it at all—giving him all the authorization he needed. It was a stupid mistake, one that he'd made before—but this time his department found out about it. Both the K9 sergeant and the lieutenant reprimanded him. "Whether he's your dog or not," he heard, meaning that, unlike the other police dogs, JJ wasn't city property, "you need our authorization on any outside call. Not only that, but from here on out you can't deploy your dog on any aggravated situations, anything that involves a weapon."

Serio's mistake now kept him from working JJ on a large number of the crimes committed on the graveyard shift. He could still respond with his dog on misdemeanors and certain felonies, but if a weapon potentially was involved—gun, knife, bat—he had to leave his bloodhound in the car. The other K9 officers handled those cases with their German shepherds. Score one for the "floppy-eared dog that doesn't bite" argument. JJ was a nonbiting dog, so he wasn't a weapon. Since Serio worked him on a leash, his hands weren't as free to use his weapon himself. The argument ran that Serio and his dog were basically defenseless while pursuing an armed criminal with no backup, as was often the case.

The argument had some justification. Tracking armed criminals is a dangerous profession. K9 officers, in particular, with or without biting dogs, are generally more vulnerable than other officers. Some statistics indicate that K9 officers are ten times more likely to be wounded in the line of duty. Dogs and their handlers are at the front end of the pursuit and often encounter armed suspects first. If the suspect decides to fight, you want a dog that bites rather than one that doesn't. The counterargument, of course, is the ability to find the suspect in the first place.

Serio had no doubt that concerns for his safety exclusively did not lie behind the motivation for limiting JJ's deployment opportunities. Despite his successes and the signed agreement, some officers maintained that JJ wasn't a real police dog. Serio could handle that. Given enough time, they would see JJ's growing track record of successes. The less charitable possibility was that JJ's successes were causing his restriction. If so, that left him with little he could do. Either way, Serio had to obey the new policy.

Soon after the new arrangement took effect, Serio responded to an armed robbery call ripe for a tracking dog. Another K9 officer got to the scene with his German shepherd around the same time. The suspects were reported to have guns, so Serio had to leave JJ in the car while he ran behind the K9 team as two-legged backup. When a weapon was involved and other K9 officers responded to the scene, he backed off. But if Serio and JJ happened to be the only dog team around, which wasn't uncommon, he wasn't about to leave the dog in the car—no matter what the suspect might be carrying.

"Most of the time," Serio said, "I definitely didn't do what I was told."

EXPRESSION

The expression is noble and dignified, and characterized by solemnity, wisdom, and power.

May 2001

City police officers were looking for suspects involved in two separate robberies at a 7-Eleven on consecutive nights. After the first night JJ tracked to a house and located the majority of the stolen beer, but the only individual there, caught trying to run out the back door, didn't match the 7-Eleven clerk's description. On the next night Serio was driving to check an address frequented by members of the Tongan Crip Gang. At least twenty-five males were partying and drinking beer in the field behind the house. Serio passed slowly and made eye contact with a man who fit the description of both robberies. The man and two others ran and jumped into a nearby yard. Serio found them hiding in the bushes and brought them out front.

Officers Daniel Delka, Russell Bartlett, Bryce Johnson, and Patti Roberts, along with K9 Aldo, responded to the scene. The officers had the three handcuffed suspects sit on the curb while they waited for another officer to retrieve an eyewitness to the theft and for a crime lab officer to take photos and fingerprints. While they waited the rest of the gang members from the party arrived and became aggressive toward the police officers, hurling obscenities and insults. Because of the threat of the approaching gang members, the officers split into two groups. Serio, Johnson, and Bartlett attempted to move the group back.

John Afoka, one of the more belligerent members of the uncooperative group, said the officers had no right to detain his friends. The officers explained why they were detaining the suspects and instructed the group to leave the area. After more yelling and unfriendly hand gestures, the group slowly walked back toward the house. Afoka turned back to the officers and said, "I'm going to shoot your ass."

A few minutes later officers heard five shots come from the field behind the house. Some of the officers hit the ground and drew their weapons, while others ran between the houses toward the direction of the shots. All the officers at the scene believed the shots were directed right at them. Johnson saw a purple Geo Storm driving through the field tearing up the grass before hitting the road at high speed. A vehicle pursuit ensued, leaving only Delka, Roberts, and a crime lab officer at the scene with the three suspects. The remaining gang members returned and continued their threats. Roberts threatened back, saying she would release her German shepherd unless they backed off. Still inside the K9 truck, Aldo was barking furiously. But it was too dangerous to remain in the area, so Delka loaded up all three suspects in the back of his patrol car, and the officers left.

Johnson's Chevy Lumina had considerably more horsepower than the Geo Storm he was pursuing. He chased the Storm until it stopped and the three suspects inside bailed and ran. Officers caught one of them in a short foot pursuit, but the other two escaped. A short time later Roberts caught one of the two running out of the neighborhood. Johnson arrived to identify him and took him into custody. The third suspect remained at large.

Serio scented JJ off the inside of the abandoned Storm, and Roberts and K9 Aldo ran behind them. JJ tracked through the neighborhood and west through some junkyards and a large field. Battling allergies, he kept sneezing but moved with purpose. The trail crossed over three barbed wire fences and led to behind the property of the US Welding Facility. JJ pulled Serio to a stand of small trees with a large tarp over them. It looked to be an old transient camp. Beneath the tarp, Serio found a man pretending to be asleep, but the performance ultimately wasn't convincing. He was sweating, breathing heavily, and his hands were bleeding from the barbed wire fences. JJ bayed at him, and Serio recognized him. It was John Afoka, the young man who had threatened to shoot them. The clerk at the 7-Eleven later identified him as one of the beer thieves, but now he faced much bigger charges.

The K9 sergeant wasn't working that night, but Serio clearly violated the policy of not deploying JJ in aggravated situations involving a weapon. Finding the guy who threatened and shot at a group of police officers, however, probably got him a free pass. That wasn't always the case. His K9 sergeant chewed out Serio on more than one occasion. After each time, he held JJ back from tracking armed offenders for a little while before responding once again to all situations where the suspect ran and his bloodhound could help find him.

The tension within the Salt Lake City K9 community ebbed and flowed for years to come. While JJ's detractors commonly cited the questionable usefulness of a bloodhound for police work, Serio believed early on that much of the opposition was directed toward him. "Not only am I not from Utah," Serio said, "I'm a new officer, and I'm five foot five. If I were six foot five, this would all have gone over a lot smoother."

What helped solidify a working partnership within Salt Lake's K9 ranks were the joint deployments of bloodhound and German shepherd. Each had their strengths, and when they pursued a suspect together, the petty squabbles went by the wayside. Perhaps Aristotle said it best: "A common danger unites even the bitterest of enemies."

Officer Cale Lennberg had a dog named Elvis—black and tan, barrel-chested, with perfectly pointy, conical ears, Elvis looked like a poster dog for the German shepherd breed. Not just a pretty face, he had trained in patrol and narcotics searches, and he could use either his nose or teeth to get the job done. Elvis also made for a good judge of character. He and JJ had teamed up together to catch four different criminals in separate incidents in 2001. Out one night in January 2002, the dogs were helping Lennberg and Serio look for a suspect who had fled from the Utah Highway Patrol after being stopped for a traffic violation.

At 1:17 a.m. the UHP pulled over Joshua Wilson, a very fit twenty-two-year-old, for driving with an expired registration. When the officer asked for identification, Wilson said he didn't have any with him. When asked for his name, his answer contained neither the word Joshua nor Wilson. The officer had Wilson step out of the car and accompany him to his patrol car while he verified the false name via the on-board computer. But Wilson didn't wait around to find out what the computer had to say about his pseudonym. He bolted. The officer called in the dogs, and Salt Lake City's finest arrived in under ten minutes.

The suspect's abandoned car sat in front of the Highway Patrol cruiser off the side of a six-lane freeway. Serio scented JJ from where the suspect had taken off, and Lennberg floated around the area in his car with Elvis while he listened to Serio and JJ's progress on the radio. It was a balmy twenty-two degrees Fahrenheit that night, and intermittent layers of thin ice lay in patches along the roads and sidewalks. JJ took Serio east along the bank of the freeway that cut through an industrial sector on the southern end of the city. They made it about two blocks when a radio update reported that the suspect had been seen in a neighborhood seven blocks farther east from where JJ was headed. Lennberg and Elvis zoomed to the new location while Serio and JJ scrambled up the icy banks of the freeway back to their car.

Lennberg, closer to six foot five than to Serio's five foot five, arrived at the last known location and started working Elvis to pick up a track. Working the graveyard shift in a neighborhood with little to no vehicle or foot traffic means that the trail of an adrenaline-charged individual passing through can stand out like a beacon to a trained dog nose. Elvis picked up a trail that led through the neighborhood of tightly spaced houses to the front porch of a one-story bungalow. Before they arrived, though, Wilson jumped off the porch and ran. It would have been the perfect time to release Elvis to give chase, but Lennberg couldn't let his dog go. So far they knew only that the suspect had fled from a traffic stop, certainly not grounds enough to release the dog to bite him. They hadn't yet learned that Wilson was on probation, wanted for a felony warrant for possession of a controlled substance, and also—the kicker—for homicide.

Holding onto Elvis's leash, Lennberg ran after Wilson. Before gaining any ground, though, he slipped on the ice and banged himself up pretty badly. Wilson disappeared. Hurt but even more pissed off, Lennberg tried to pick up a track with Elvis where he'd last seen the suspect. He hadn't been able to find a solid lead when Serio and JJ arrived.

Without a whiff of K9 rivalry, Lennberg wanted them to find the guy; he didn't care who got the credit. When they learned over the radio exactly whom they were following, Lennberg *really* wanted to find the guy. If he saw him again, he now had a green light to release Elvis.

After a few minutes of searching, JJ picked up a track heading south on 200 East Street. The trail cut through an alley, across the next street, and back again farther down 200 East. JJ passed a garage behind a house, stopped abruptly, and did an about face. He tracked right to the detached garage and lifted his head, whipping his nose back and forth, doing the Stevie Wonder, bouncing around the scent cloud. He zeroed in on a tall, thin tree next to the garage and bayed up into the air.

By then the cavalry had arrived. Lennberg and Elvis stood behind Serio, multiple UHP officers stood nearby, and Salt Lake City patrol and Metro Gang Unit officers joined the party. Serio looked back at the sea of blue uniforms and said, "He's indicating that our guy's up there."

They all looked back at him with a collective expression of *How the fuck are we going to check up there?* It was dark, and the roof of the garage was about twelve feet up.

Serio handed JJ's leash to one of the officers and climbed the tree. The top of the garage lay only two feet away, and Serio easily stepped onto the roof. Wilson was lying there, flat as possible. Gun in hand, Serio pounced on him right away, not wanting to take any chances of a third pursuit. He handcuffed him without resistance, and the fire department came with a ladder.

"We're going to have to uncuff him to get him down," Serio said, looking at the steep angle of the ladder. "It's too dangerous." He worried about releasing Wilson again. It was still just the two of them on the roof. But with so many cops below, Serio was pretty sure that Wilson wouldn't try anything. Besides, Elvis was down there waiting, ready to chew him up if necessary.

"I can walk down with my handcuffs," Wilson said. "I used to be a roofer. It's a piece of cake for me." Face forward, hands cuffed behind his back, he descended the ladder as easily as a flight of steps.

•••

Two weeks later the opening ceremonies of the Salt Lake City Winter Olympics began with the Mormon Tabernacle Choir

singing the "Star-Spangled Banner" and LeAnn Rimes perform-
ing "Light the Fire Within," the official song of the games. Highlights of the following sixteen days included the men's Canadian
ice hockey team defeating the Americans in the final—their first
hockey gold in fifty years—sixteen-year-old Sarah Hughes winning gold in figure skating over her heavily favored American
teammate, Michelle Kwan, and a bloodhound named JJ sniffing
out thirty-seven-year-old Eric Strothers from his hiding spot to
be charged with a drug offense and interfering with police.

To call the police presence heavy during the Olympics in Salt
Lake would be an understatement. Held only five months after
the September 11 terrorist attacks, the Olympics qualified as a
National Special Security Event. The US Secret Service managed
event security, the FBI handled intelligence and counterterror-
ism, and the US Marine Corps handled aerial surveillance and
regional radar control. The handlers of the Salt Lake City K9
Squad all went on patrol to add more bodies in blue to the vast
security detail, which included additional officers from across
the country as well as from select international law enforcement
agencies.

Unlike the athletes, JJ didn't get to exercise his legs as much
as usual during the Olympics. Other than finding Eric Strothers, it was a slow two and a half weeks for JJ, and he got to
catch up on a lot of missed sleep. He was going to need it. The
night after the closing ceremonies, JJ tracked down two of three
suspects who bailed out of a stolen car pursued by police and
scrambled in different directions. Fleeing suspects tend to shed
their clothes when running from the police. The logic holds that
they don't want to be caught wearing an outfit that matches a
witness's description. But with a scent dog on your trail, it's best
to keep everything on.

JJ scented off an abandoned jacket and led to one suspect hiding in a building. After handing the suspect over to another officer, Serio brought JJ back to the car to start a new track looking for one of the other suspects. JJ found a ski mask on the ground and, after following a trail over fences and into another neighborhood, located the second suspect hiding beneath a tree. The two suspects gave up the third, and police found him at his home pretending to be asleep.

A worrier in general, Serio always looked over his shoulder, wondering if the bloodhound program was going to get the ax. Later that spring he received news that should have wiped such worries away. Serio received Salt Lake City's Police Officer of the Year award, an honor bestowed on less than one half of 1 percent of Salt Lake City officers throughout their careers. JJ's record for 2001, with twenty-one criminal apprehensions and ten evidence finds to his credit, eventually tied for the lowest annual total in his career.

By 2002, after a one-year trial period and another year as an official member of the K9 Squad, JJ had hit his stride. Although animosity and competition with the German shepherd handlers continued to oscillate, JJ's list of supporters in influential positions had grown. The glowing media attention didn't hurt, either. Serio would never admit it, but JJ's job security never looked so solid.

Two years into police work, JJ had certainly been around the block, but nowhere near enough to have seen it all. His potential to find missing persons had helped land the initial trial run and came up again in support of making him an official member of the K9 Squad. But so far, while he had worked a number of cases involving missing kids or the elderly, they were always found by others, usually at a neighbor's house or walking blocks away.

In November 2000 JJ helped search for a man with Alzheimer's who had wandered off from his home. Grateful when her husband was found, the man's wife wrote a letter to the chief of police, thanking Serio and JJ for their concern and diligence. But there was nothing sensational about the track, and it didn't receive any media attention.

JJ's next missing person case was a different story.

WEIGHT

The mean average weight of adult dogs, in fair condition, is 90 pounds. Dogs attain the weight of 110 pounds. The greater weights are to be preferred, provided (as in the case of height) that quality and proportion are also combined.

June 2002

"An SLCPD bloodhound named J.J. picked up Elizabeth's scent . . . leading up to Tomahawk Drive in the circle above the backyard, but then the trail apparently went cold."

So say Tom Smart and Lee Benson in their book *In Plain Sight: The Startling Truth Behind the Elizabeth Smart Investigation*. But that's not the startling truth of what happened on JJ's track in the hours immediately following her abduction at knifepoint from her bedroom. JJ did pick up Elizabeth's scent, but the trail didn't go cold.

• • •

At the 7-Eleven on 800 South and 1300 East, two men came into the store, grabbed a case of Milwaukee's Best, and ran off without paying into the early morning hours of Wednesday, June 5. Serio and Officer Jason Hathaway arrived several minutes later. It was a common enough occurrence, but it baffled Serio that the shoplifters always took the cheap beer. "If you're going to steal, why not steal the good stuff?"

With him that morning in his police truck, Serio had JJ and Josie, his other bloodhound. Josie was two years old and, according to Lisa, "*her* baby." They got her as a puppy, and as with JJ she was intended exclusively as a family pet. For the most part she still was, but Serio wanted to train Josie as a backup in case JJ ever got injured. Responding to the beer theft, Serio got JJ out and started a track, but it was a short one. The suspects likely got in a car around the corner and were long gone. Just as Serio and Hathaway were wrapping up the call, they heard a triple beep from dispatch signaling a high-priority event in progress.

"Kidnapping just occurred. Complainant's fourteen-year-old daughter was taken from her bedroom at gunpoint approximately three hours ago."

Just two miles away, Serio, his two bloodhounds, and Hathaway were about as close as you could be to the address without actually being in the neighborhood.

"Kilo 855, copy?" asked the dispatcher, using Serio's call sign. "Kidnapping just occurred."

"Kilo 855, I'm en route to that."

Serio knew that 99 percent of these types of calls eventually revealed themselves either as family custody disputes—when a parent took the kid when he or she wasn't supposed to—or rebellious young love, when the girl is out with a boyfriend, and rules don't apply to two people so perfectly meant for each other. It could be a 1 percent case, a true kidnapping. "Everything goes through your head," Serio said. Driving in separate vehicles, he and Hathaway got to the house in five minutes. Arriving shortly after 4:00 a.m., Serio and Hathaway were the third and fourth officers on the scene.

The Smarts' 4,400-square-foot house lay at the northeast end of a cul-de-sac in the affluent Federal Heights neighborhood, a steep tract of land above the University of Utah that climbs the foothills of the Wasatch Mountains and offers expansive views of the Salt Lake Valley.

JJ was still wearing his harness from the track at the 7-Eleven, so he was ready to go. Serio asked Sergeant Brian Bailey, senior officer at the scene, to get him something with Elizabeth's scent on it, a pillowcase or clothing that she had recently worn. He was hoping that JJ would be able to get a good, strong odor and sort through the contaminated scene, with its intermingled smells from two parents, four siblings, multiple police officers, and a growing number of neighbors showing up to help search for the fourteen-year-old girl with short blonde hair, last known to be wearing red pajamas.

Sergeant Bailey gave Serio a white cotton-knit sweater that Elizabeth had worn the day before. Serio and JJ started at the back of the house beside a chair apparently used by the suspect to get into the kitchen window. The screen had been cut with a knife. Serio scented JJ off Elizabeth's sweater and commanded, "Go find!" Officer Hathaway followed as backup.

JJ picked up a track heading southeast along the side of the house and looped back around to the front driveway. He stopped, lifted his head up, and looked left and right. Serio had seen the body language hundreds of times. Not only could Serio see it, he could feel it on the other end of the leash. JJ had lost the track. Serio thought JJ might have missed a turn and brought him back to the southeast side of the house. JJ hooked into the track again, this time working slowly and deliberately. Because JJ didn't lock into it immediately, Serio knew that the trail wasn't fresh. An older track matched the approximate three-hour time lapse.

JJ slowly followed a short stepping-stone path behind the house that ended where the stones met a narrow dirt path probably created by deer that often ventured into the neighborhood to eat prized daylilies and other floral treats.

By the time he hit the dirt path, JJ was excited. He bayed and picked up speed. Southeast of the house the path rose sharply up a hill pocked with shrubs and intermittently rimmed with pines, juniper, and scrub oak. Well beyond the periphery of the house, everything was pitch dark. Along the track Serio's flashlight revealed ground disturbance on the grass and dirt indicating that one or more individuals had walked the route lately. Hot on the trail, JJ pulled up the hill next to a vacant lot at 1600 East Tomahawk Drive. At the top of the lot, JJ alerted on a big area of bushes and trees. He detailed the ground, methodically sniffing the thick cluster of vegetation. Punctuating the night with periodic bays, JJ was indicating that something was there.

In an extensive study of 775 child abduction murder cases across the country, researchers found that, in 76 percent of cases, the child was dead within three hours of abduction. If this was a legitimate kidnapping and potential murder case, the victim's body might be lying in the bushes where JJ was sniffing. While he searched with his flashlight, he let his dog detail the bushes until they both realized nothing was there. JJ was stuck and couldn't find an odor trail leading out. Serio pulled him away. A few feet farther up the hill, they came to Tomahawk Drive.

Serio tried to get JJ to reacquire the scent trail, but they had just come from a vegetation-rich surface to hard asphalt. Imagine following a wide country path to a dead end and learning that a human hair lying somewhere nearby points the way. Serio had been in this type of situation with JJ before, and he was doing everything his training had taught to help the dog find the right trail. Then officers at the Smart house, four hundred yards below, called on the radio and told him about some large stone ovens beyond Tomahawk Drive farther up the hill. "Go check up there. That would be a good place for kids to go hang out or for a kidnapper to take someone." Thinking that JJ might have lost the scent at Tomahawk Drive because the suspect and victim had gotten into a car, he pulled JJ away from where he wanted to stay. They headed up the hill to search the kilns.

Settlers of the Salt Lake Valley built the historic limekilns in the 1850s for cooking limestone deposits at exceedingly high temperatures to make lime powder for cement, mortar, and plaster. The kilns lie at the bottom of a gulch and, being at least three hundred yards from the nearest street or residence, make an ideal spot for anyone not wanting to be disturbed.

Fifty feet wide and about twenty feet tall, the limekilns' outer walls consist of gray stone. Ash-covered brick lines the chimneys inside. Four arched openings, the oven doors, adorn the front, and the back of the structure extends into the side of the mountain. It's a historic site that you might travel to see but that on arrival might make you wonder why you bothered in the first place. Serio felt the same way. They searched all around the kilns for about twenty minutes and got nothing. Serio brought JJ back down. He thought there was a good possibility that the suspect had parked a car on Tomahawk Drive and taken off with Elizabeth from there. Still, he went yard to yard along Tomahawk, casting JJ in all directions.

More and more people had arrived at the Smart house, and Serio was hearing increased chatter on the air about all kinds of different leads. The media had arrived in droves, and the police already were getting calls from citizens wanting to be helpful, saying they might have seen her here or there. An early wacko—one of many to come—had called, claiming to have Elizabeth and wanting a ransom of ten million dollars.

Some detectives at the scene, doing the best they could with an increasing flood of conflicting information, thought the suspect had taken Elizabeth around the front of the house and gotten into a car farther down the street. Serio had his doubts about that. Since he'd been tracking with JJ, they'd received information provided by Mary Katherine, Elizabeth's nine-year-old sister who shared a bedroom with her and had witnessed the kidnapping. She initially got up to tell her parents when she thought it was safe but saw the kidnapper down the hall with Elizabeth outside her brother's room. Scared he might return for her, she went back to her bed and pretended to be asleep. Obviously terrified, she didn't notify her parents that Elizabeth had been taken until more than two hours had passed. Mary Katherine told investigators that the man who took Elizabeth told her sister to put on her shoes before they left the bedroom. A little while later, she heard them walking outside below her bedroom window. It sounded to her as if they'd gone around the front of the house.

Detectives cited the information from Mary Katherine, as well as the logic of what a typical kidnapper would do, to conjecture that the suspect had gotten into a car out front and driven away. Serio was focused on the information about the shoes. It wouldn't make sense for the kidnapper to take the time for Elizabeth to put on her shoes if he was just going to put her in a car. It would make sense, however, if they were going to hike for a bit. The trail that JJ took behind the house leading up to Tomahawk Drive was too rocky and rough for bare feet.

Serio was still casting JJ in the yards along Tomahawk and eventually got back to the cluster of trees and bushes where his bloodhound had lost the scent. They proceeded a few yards farther east, and then JJ picked up a new track, cautiously following an asphalt path that extended beyond the end of Tomahawk Drive. By the time he got to the end of the path, he started moving fast. They headed east along the trail and passed just below the Block U, a hundred-foot concrete letter U that lies against the side of Mount Van Cott, overlooking the University of Utah campus and the Salt Lake Valley below. The Block U, outlined with 240 lights that alternate red and white, lights up during home games, and according to custom, "its lights flash in victory and burn steady even in defeat." No lights were on as JJ and Serio passed thirty yards beneath it.

JJ followed the trail along the side of the mountain, another neighborhood with large houses to his right. Over a hill the trail descended to the south then west for about a hundred yards, where it merged with the Bonneville Shoreline Trail, a popular route for hiking and mountain biking. To the right the trail leads to another neighborhood and the University of Utah campus below. To the left the trail leads straight up into a canyon. Not wavering, JJ turned left. That didn't make sense to Serio. He looked at Hathaway, still following them, who agreed with Serio. Civilization and a good chance to escape lay to the right. To the left lay steep mountains and unforgiving terrain.

Serio pulled JJ back and forced him to circle around at the split, making sure he checked both directions. He wanted his dog to go to the right. JJ checked that direction, didn't find anything, swung back to the left, and bayed, eager to keep going. Serio followed but shook his head.

"This isn't making a lot of sense," he said to Hathaway.

"No," said Hathaway, "I don't think so either."

At the command post back at the Smarts' house, Homicide Detective Kelly Kent and her partner, Cordon Parks, were listening to Serio and JJ's progress over the air. Other investigators at the scene supported the theory that Elizabeth had been taken in a car. They thought Serio and his bloodhound were on a wild goose chase, but Kent and Parks argued otherwise. "The dog has no bias. He's not prejudiced by logic. He's going up the hill; let him go up the hill. Shut up, and stop telling him where to go."

Serio let JJ lead but slowed their pace to confer with Hathaway. They both decided that, even though it didn't make sense for a kidnapper to take someone up into the canyon, they weren't going to abandon the track until they could get a helicopter in the air and have it take a look. Serio called dispatch from the radio on his chest. "Can we get a state chopper up here to canvas the hillside?"

Serio knew dogs, but Hathaway knew helicopters. In addition to being a Salt Lake City patrol officer, Hathaway was training to be a helicopter pilot with the Utah National Guard. Hathaway requested that the helicopter have a forward looking infrared system (FLIR), a thermal imaging camera mounted on the helicopter that can detect infrared radiation. Connected to a display in the helicopter cockpit, the camera can pick up heat emitted by the human body and works especially well in cold temperatures.

Sunrise that morning came at 5:57 a.m., but on the western side of the Wasatch Mountain Range they couldn't yet see the dawn. The northeastern canyon where they were headed, known as Dry Creek Canyon, was still dark, and the temperature, around sixty degrees, remained cold enough for the FLIR system to be effective. The temperature later in the day rose to eighty-four degrees, too warm for the thermal camera to differentiate warm bodies from the heat of the ground and the surrounding atmosphere saturated by solar loading. When they called for the helicopter, Serio thought, from prior experience, that they'd have to wait forty-five minutes to an hour before it arrived.

Salt Lake County had recently eliminated its helicopter program, turning everything over to the Utah Highway Patrol. When UHP got the request, they fired up the helicopter in under five minutes. At the Smart house Sergeant Bailey was following the radio traffic and talked to the dispatcher. "Have UHP notify us when they are in the air so we can set up a marker." This told Serio and Hathaway to keep their flashlights on.

"UHP chopper in the air," the dispatcher called; "ETA two to five minutes."

The rapid response amazed Serio. He and Hathaway had continued up the trail. Baying and pulling hard, JJ wanted to keep going, hot on something. Steep and gravely, lined with scrub oak and Rocky Mountain maple, the trail followed a narrow, winding creek bed higher up into the mountains. For mountain bikers this part of the trail was the hard investment before the payoff of majestic views up top and the rapid roller-coaster descent back down. Serio slowed JJ down once again when he heard the helicopter approaching from the west and looked for an open area away from the trees so the pilot could easily spot them.

The helicopter pilot used the infrared camera to clear the area around the limekilns first, double-checking that nothing was there, then approached Serio and Hathaway's position, looking for the beams of their flashlights. The thermal scanning technology showed two police officers, one short and one tall, and a hot bloodhound itching to keep going. The pilot had switched to the officers' radio channel so they could communicate directly.

The helicopter now directly above, Serio said, "My dog is telling me there's something up ahead. Can you check the canyon northeast of our location?"

The helicopter proceeded slowly up the canyon while Serio, Hathaway, and JJ waited.

A short time later the pilot called over the radio, "I've got two joggers up here, male and female, about a half mile from your location."

"Are you sure they're joggers?" Serio asked.

"Typical jogging attire, running shoes. Running together on trail that switches back west across the mountain. Looks like a good possibility that's what your dog is following. I'm not seeing anybody else up here."

"Can he really make sure this canyon is clear?" Serio asked Hathaway.

"This thing can spot a rabbit in the dark," Hathaway replied. "Its sphere is pretty accurate and can cover a wide range. It should be able to spot a human up there easily."

The helicopter kept scanning, overlapping the searched area, still on the hunt for human life. After a few minutes the pilot called again: "There's nothing up here but those two joggers."

Baying, JJ wanted up that hill. Reluctant to leave the track, Serio let him go for another 150 yards and watched his body language closely, checking to see if anything changed. Nothing did. JJ kept going strong. From his experience Serio knew that even the best tracking dog can switch midway through a track to follow a new scent. Some twenty to thirty minutes had lapsed between JJ's original track up to Tomahawk Drive and the secondary track he picked up there after they came down from the limekilns. Serio worried that JJ might have taken up a new scent trail because he knew Serio wanted him to find something.

The sun was rising over the mountains, and more leads were pouring over the airwaves. Serio hesitated to pull his dog off the track, but eventually, he reached a point where he hesitated more to keep going. He had to preserve JJ's energy if he wanted to keep him working and pursue what now appeared to be more viable leads. JJ might have missed a turn, and a lot more places needed searching. It seemed possible that JJ was tracking the two joggers up ahead. The helicopter had cleared the canyon of other people, and Serio and Hathaway kept coming back to the conclusion that it didn't make sense for a kidnapper to take a victim so far away on foot into rugged mountains.

Serio pulled on JJ's leash and stopped him. "Come on, Jay, we're going back."

JJ gave him a funny look, one that Serio had seen before. It read: *I'm not done yet. Why are we stopping?*

If I pulled him off the right track, I'll never live it down, Serio thought as they made their way back down the canyon. Along with Hathaway, he and JJ searched the yards and interiors of some large houses under construction, thinking them good places for a kidnapper to take a victim. Nearing the Smart house and hearing that more investigators at the scene speculated that the suspect had taken Elizabeth in a car parked nearby, Serio grew more confident that JJ was tracking the joggers. By the time they returned to Tomahawk Drive, the neighborhood was swarming with people looking for Elizabeth. Officers were going door to door, neighbors and family members called out her name, and a number of search-and-rescue handlers had arrived with their dogs. JJ was tired out, and Serio had to let him rest. He told one of the search-and-rescue handlers, a woman with a German shepherd, that if she was looking for a place to start searching, he suggested going up the Bonneville Shoreline Trail.

Back at his truck Serio gave JJ some food and much-needed rest. But not taking time to rest himself, he got Josie out, put on her harness, and started working his second bloodhound. He started her behind the Smarts' house, the same place he'd started JJ. She followed the exact same path up to Tomahawk Drive. That didn't surprise him. She naturally would have followed the same path as JJ, likely picking up his scent along with the search scent.

Meanwhile, tips came flooding in from concerned citizens all over the place. People reported potential sightings far and wide and found clothing in their yards that wasn't theirs. Serio took Josie to leads that directed them to search south of the house through neighborhoods and hiking trails cutting through a ravine that led down to Popperton Park and Shriners Hospital. Serio worked until Josie was worn out. Sometime after 10:00 a.m. they packed up and went home.

What soon became one of the largest manhunts in US history had only just begun.

• • •

Only a month before Elizabeth was abducted, Utah adopted the Rachael Alert, named after three-year-old Rachael Runyan, abducted and murdered in 1982. The alert system, which later became the national Amber Alert, is a rapid-response network supported by a partnership with law enforcement and media broadcasters to alert the public when a child is abducted. The Elizabeth Smart case was the first time the alert had been used in Utah. In the days immediately following her abduction, thousands of volunteers joined the search with civilian search-and-rescue organizations and local, state, and federal law enforcement agencies. The extended Smart family worked tirelessly to help the search efforts and made sure that the case remained a top news story, agreeing to all interview requests and providing twice-daily press briefings.

Two weeks after the abduction, Serio was called to assist the FBI at the Smart house. The federal investigators had called in a group of dog handlers from the Los Angeles County Sheriff's Office that specialized in scent identification. Serio described what JJ did and showed them his first track up to Tomahawk Drive and the secondary track into Dry Creek Canyon. He hoped that the Southern California dog teams could perform a miracle where he and JJ couldn't. Serio accompanied them in searching some nearby houses that the FBI was investigating. They found no trails or tangible leads.

• • •

While the search for Elizabeth Smart was ongoing, Serio and JJ continued their criminal-catching ways. A freshly minted Officer of the Year, Serio and his bloodhound completed another stellar year apprehending thieves, carjackers, armed robbers, and other nefarious sorts. In one notable case JJ tracked a man who fled from a stolen vehicle and disappeared into an apartment building. The man knocked on a resident's door and said, "Let me in, or something bad will happen to you." The frightened woman let him in. JJ brought Serio up the stairwell to the second floor and narrowed the search to one of two apartment doors situated close together. The suspect was found, and the woman was unharmed.

In the early afternoon of March 12, 2003, in the backyard of his new house, Serio was raking rocks out of the dirt in preparation for laying sod so JJ would have a nice place to run and play. Lisa called from the back patio. "Hey, Mike, they found Elizabeth Smart."

Elizabeth had been found, along with her captors, Brian David Mitchell and Wanda Barzee, in Sandy, Utah, about twenty miles south of her home. Like the rest of Utah and the millions nationwide who had followed the case, Serio rejoiced at the news. Two other highly publicized child abduction cases the year before, both in California, ended in the death of the victims. Missing for over nine months and found alive, Elizabeth Smart had defied the odds and rejoined her family. The details of where she had been taken the night of her abduction quickly emerged. When Serio heard, his stomach sank, and he felt sick, unsure that he wanted to continue working—not just in K9 but as a police officer at all.

The FBI, along with Salt Lake City police investigators, including Cordon Parks and Kelly Kent, interviewed Elizabeth about the night of her abduction. They showed her a map of the area around her house so she could point out, to the best of her recollection, the path she followed after being taken from her house at knifepoint. She described walking up a trail behind the house leading toward Tomahawk Drive. Just before getting there, they saw a car parked with its engine running in the circle at the end of Tomahawk. A private security car had stopped to write a report. Mitchell made her hide with him in the thick bushes just below the street and waited until the car drove off. It was the same set of bushes where JJ had spent so much time detailing the ground.

The human body constantly sheds pheromones and cells from the skin, respiratory tract, and digestive tract. If you stay in one place, whether for two minutes or twenty, your scent pools, drifting in a pocket of air and concentrating along the ground all around you. Even after you leave, your lingering scent can be so strong that a dog can think you're still right there. JJ couldn't pick up the scent line out of the bushes and initially lost the trail. He reacquired a new scent trail just east of the bushes approximately twenty-five minutes later, after Serio had been told to search the limekilns.

From the bushes Elizabeth and Mitchell walked east past the end of Tomahawk and then, as determined by investigators, along the trail beneath the Block U. On reaching the Bonneville Shoreline Trail, they turned left, away from civilization, and headed up into Dry Creek Canyon. Somewhere farther up, they turned east off the main trail and scrambled up steep terrain covered with thick brush to arrive at a well-hidden campsite cut into a hillside. The twenty-four-foot-long lean-to shelter made of eight tree posts interlocked with a roof of three-inch-diameter tree limbs, thick black plastic, and packed dirt made it hard to spot the people inside from the air, even with a specially equipped helicopter.

In the shelter Brian David Mitchell forced Elizabeth Smart to "marry" him in a false ceremony before he raped her for the first time of many over the next "nine months of hell," as Elizabeth described them. Elizabeth told investigators that, as Mitchell was taking her up the trail to the campsite that morning, she heard a single dog barking behind her.

Determining the origin and distance of sound is tricky, particularly at night over elevated terrain. The campsite lay at least another mile and a half up the canyon from where Serio stopped JJ. There's no way to know how close they made it to Elizabeth that morning. It's possible that JJ really was following the two joggers whom the helicopter spotted. Had he made it to where Mitchell and Elizabeth veered off the main trail, he might have missed the turn. But Serio doesn't think so. Even if JJ had been following the joggers, however unlikely, once the bloodhound got to the turn, he would have recognized Elizabeth's initial scent from her sweater and also picked up on the fear scent coming from her and possibly Mitchell—if he was at all concerned he might be caught.

The *if onlys* will forever plague Serio. As with any investigation that drags on with no results, critics came out of the woodwork. Both experienced and armchair dog handlers claimed, "My dog could have found her." Misguided though he thought it was, the criticism stung Serio—but nowhere near as much as the self-flagellation. Dog handlers almost never catch child abductors. Usually, too much time has passed, and the smells of family, friends, and neighbors traipsing the ground in a wide radius severely contaminate the scene. The chance of the dog's working through the contamination and finding the right trail is extremely small.

But in the Smart case they had had a shot. The time lapse had been fairly long, but her parents didn't wait to notify the police, as often happens. They called shortly after they discovered Elizabeth missing. The scent contamination occurred mostly around the house, and Serio got JJ working, because of the steep terrain, away from where the average searcher would have looked. The dirt and vegetation also helped.

Hindsight may be clear, but it comes flanked with blinders, conveniently ignoring the vast and muddled panorama of the moment. Tips and theories of Elizabeth's whereabouts were coming in from all over the place. Police officers learn to use their resources and trust them. Serio trusted his dog enough to call out a UHP helicopter to look ahead of the trail they were following. Most of the investigators that morning believed that Elizabeth had already been taken in a car. A few may have believed that JJ was on to something, Serio included, but once the report came back that the helicopter had cleared the canyon, finding only two joggers, all belief in the bloodhound's track dissipated. Technology and human logic had won the argument. Heat-seeking sensors showed nothing, and a kidnapper taking a victim high into the mountains didn't make sense to anyone—except JJ.

JJ's being pulled off the track was the first of many near misses in the extended search for Elizabeth Smart. In the days immediately following her abduction, lines of family members and thousands of volunteers searched the foothills. Elizabeth said that one day at the campsite she heard her uncles some-where nearby, calling her name. Several dog teams with search-and-rescue organizations also helped in the search.

Her uncle Tom Smart and Lee Benson didn't get all the details right about JJ in their book—they have him showing up some-time after 7:30 a.m., more than three hours after he arrived, and stop at the point where he initially lost the trail on Tomahawk Drive—but they do report another promising moment involv-ing search dogs. Three days after the kidnapping, a group of handlers and their dogs—a golden retriever named Maverick, a German shepherd named Leroy, and a bloodhound named Speed—were searching the foothills near the Bonneville Shore-line Trail. Linda Sosa, Maverick's handler, said of the three dogs, "All were on a dead run up the canyon." Linda called the search director at the coordination center based at Shriners Hospital, and he told them to come back and team up with police.

Two hours later, six police officers, two of them heavily equipped in SWAT gear, accompanied the three handlers and their dogs. The dogs picked up the trail again. After a few hours with no obvious end, the search was called off. The group reportedly stopped somewhere along Red Butte Canyon, "just one ridge south of Dry Creek Canyon." Speed, one of the three dogs on the search-and-rescue team, happened to come from a litter of puppies from Missouri. She was JJ's sister.

• • •

In May 2011, after years of stalled legal proceedings—twice deemed mentally ill and unfit to stand trial—Brian David Mitch-ell was finally sentenced to life in prison for kidnapping and rape. The lawyers for the prosecution said that the case hinged on Elizabeth Smart's brave testimony in sharing the graphic details of her nine months of captivity. Wanda Barzee, Mitchell's legal wife and accomplice, received a sentence of fifteen years in federal prison for her role in the kidnapping.

Elizabeth has become an outspoken advocate for children, speaking out across the country to raise awareness about child victimization and lobbying Congress to pass stricter laws dealing with sexual predators. Hired as an ABC News contributor on missing persons cases, Elizabeth also completed a mission in France for the Mormon Church; attended Brigham Young University, where she studied music; and recently married a Mormon man from Scotland, whom she met in Paris.

Referring to Brian David Mitchell, Elizabeth has said that her mother's best advice was, "He has taken nine months of your life that you can never get back. Don't give him another minute." She has taken that advice to heart. Speaking directly to Mitchell during his sentencing, Elizabeth said, "I want you to know that I have a wonderful life now. No matter what you do, you will never affect me again."

COLOR

The colors are black and tan, liver and tan, and red; the darker colors being sometimes interspersed with lighter or badger-colored hair, and sometimes flecked with white. A small amount of white is permissible on chest, feet, and tip of stern.

July 2003

Free from the human foibles of guilt and afterthought, JJ remained focused even after tracks led to nothing. Only three things could distract him: an empty stomach, Officer Chris Housley, or goat heads—the prickly spines of the *Tribulus terrestris* plant, also known as devil's thorn, the scourge of bicyclists and dogs with tender paws throughout the West.

Serio always had doggie treats to calm an empty stomach. Officer Housley was a little more challenging. Serio and Lisa trusted few other people to watch their dogs when they left town, and JJ loved her. If she showed up on a call where JJ was working, he pulled right off the track to go say hello. As mad as that made Serio, the goat heads posed more of a problem. Even on a hot track, JJ sometimes pulled up short and lifted his paw in the air, waiting for his partner to remove the goat head. The ten-millimeter-long spines can easily puncture a bicycle tire and have an affinity for burrowing into the pads of dogs' paws. Luckily, not every day on the job required running through unkempt yards and scraggly fields after suspects.

In addition to many other responsibilities, police officers interact with citizens in a positive way to convince them that an encounter with the police doesn't always have to be the worst part of their day. "Down on the ground!," "Hands behind your head!," and some variation of "If you run, you'll only go to jail tired" are effective under the right circumstances, but they don't go a long way toward building rapport. Public outreach missions establish trust in the police force and a sense of partnership with the communities that they serve. Since most adults have already formed their opinion of the police, a large part of what's known as community-oriented policing focuses on children.

Bloodhounds are hard to resist, and children don't even try. McGruff the Crime Dog—the iconic mascot of the National Crime Prevention Council—is, after all, a bloodhound. Clifford the Big Red Dog most closely resembles a bloodhound. The idea for him came about when an editor at Harper & Row selected a sketch by artist/author Norman Bridwell featuring a baby girl and a horse-sized bloodhound. "There might be a story in this," the editor casually remarked. A big red police dog, JJ was McGruff and Clifford rolled into one.

The Salt Lake City K9 Squad had been visiting the Shriners Hospital for Children for years. They always performed apprehension demonstrations. A police officer, probably the one who drew the short straw, stood in the middle of the south lawn behind the hospital, wearing a padded suit that made him look like the Michelin Man. The hospital staff and all the kids who could get out of bed (most of them) lined up along the hillside to watch. A K9 officer called out in a booming voice across the lawn, "Stop! Salt Lake City Police. Show me your hands!" Turning 180 degrees, the Michelin Man waddled away like a spry penguin running. Unclipped from his leash, the German shepherd ran at frightening speed and a few seconds later latched onto the man's arm, often barreling into him with enough force to knock him to the ground.

In Serio's first year on the K9 Squad, he played the Michelin Man. After he was done "catching the dog" as they call it, he got out of the suit and let the kids pet JJ. The kids could also pet the German shepherds, but their handlers had to take great care because, shockingly, kids don't always pay attention to what you tell them. With JJ Serio never had to worry. Before he knew it, kids swarmed him, reaching in to touch and grab hold of JJ. The bloodhound just lay on the ground, and twenty kids could pile on top of him. JJ happily soaked in all their love.

On one visit Serio learned from one of the staff members that a young girl who had recently had surgery couldn't leave her room. With an okay from her doctors, he brought JJ into her hospital room. Rosalia Chavez, eight years old, had come to the United States from Mexico to have surgery on her leg. She didn't speak English. Neither did JJ. They had an instant connection. Rosalia's face lit up at the sight of the big hound in her room. The K9 Squad gave her a German shepherd stuffed animal, but JJ didn't hold that against her. Tail wagging, he laid his head across her shoulder and sniffed gently at her face. Grinning from ear to ear, she patted him softly on the head and didn't seem to mind the slobber.

Visits to elementary schools around Salt Lake City were always louder. The "auditorium" was usually just a small wooden stage in the cafeteria: tables temporarily replaced with plastic chairs. Chris Ward and his German shepherd Rosco started the assembly off. He set up a drug-sniffing demonstration on the stage, hiding the contraband in one of half a dozen backpacks and luggage bags spread in a line. "Which one is it?" Ward asked the kids, and they yelled out their picks. Jazzed up from the noise bouncing off the cafeteria walls, Rosco worked at a frenzied pace, sniffing the air back and forth until he found his mark. Once he started scratching at the right bag, alerting on the drugs, Rosco got his reward, and the kids all clapped and cheered. But they were waiting for the bloodhound.

Only a few people in the world have ever experienced what JJ did when he walked into an auditorium packed with hundreds of kids. Paul, John, George, and Ringo might have understood, but the rest of us have to imagine it. The kids jumped up and down to get a look, laughed at the shake of his head, and went berserk at the first sound out of his mouth. Climbing onto

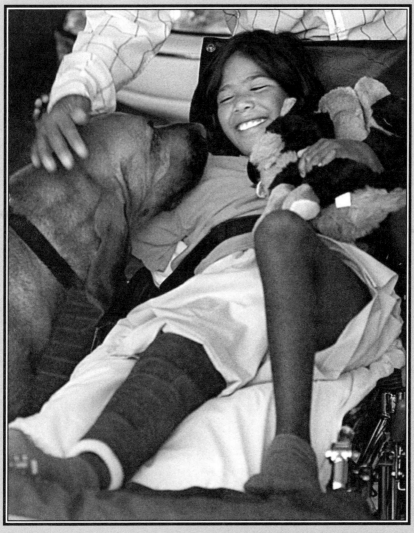

JJ comforts 8-year-old Rosalia Chavez at Shriners Hospital for Children.
*Photograph courtesy of Laura Seitz/*Deseret News

the stage with JJ, Serio gave Ward one of JJ's jerky treats. Ward waved the treat in front of JJ's face and ran off the stage. Held back by Serio, JJ lifted his head and bayed to the rafters. The kids roared. Still running, Ward ran through and looped around the crowd. Serio let JJ go. He took off, his nails clacking against the tile floor, but you couldn't hear it for all the commotion. JJ's bays, however, continued to rise above the din, and he quickly caught up to Ward, throwing his paws on the K9 officer's shoulders and bathing him with slobbery bloodhound love. Ward happily surrendered and gave JJ his treat.

"Do it again! Do it again!" everyone said at schools, churches, and scout troops throughout the city. Afterward, the kids could encounter the star of the show, hands reaching through the crowd just to touch JJ's fur. Swarmed again, he didn't mind. He knew if it got too out of hand, his security detail would come rescue him from his adoring fans.

Not every demonstration with school kids was an unqualified success, though. One of Serio's neighbors, a teacher, asked if he would come show her sixth graders some of JJ's tracking skills. Outside the school Serio selected an eager volunteer and told him, "Go down to the pavilion, take a right, pick a tree, and hide." He also told the teacher to keep her eyes on the kid, chuckling, "I don't want to lose anyone." The pavilion lay on school grounds, as did the trees Serio had in mind where the boy would hide. Immediately west of the trees lay Murray City Park, a sprawling urban green space with multiple athletic fields, playgrounds, picnic sites, outdoor amphitheater, outdoor swimming pool, outdoor ice-skating rink, creek, and hiking trails through an arboretum and other wooded areas.

"Do you want to go to *work*?" Serio asked JJ, showing the kids how he readied his dog to track. He scented JJ off the kid's hat, and they were off. An entire class of sixth graders and two teachers followed in their wake. JJ turned right around the pavilion, passed the trees without a pause, and entered Murray Park. The boy was nowhere to be seen and a long way to be smelled. Serio began to worry but said nothing. JJ kept searching, taking Serio and the class far into the park. Earning an A for effort, the kid had done his best to make the trail as complicated as possible. JJ took them back and forth, winding through all the park's numerous amenities. Incredibly stressed, Serio was sweating up a storm. The kids were having a blast, though. A walk in the park beat quadratic equations any day of the week. The teachers may well have agreed. It took a long time, but they eventually found the dedicated fugitive on the other side of Murray Park. Serio wanted to wring his neck, but JJ had only love in his heart. He licked the boy, delighted in his find.

"I learned, when you do demos, you always set them up in a controlled situation for success," Serio said. "Otherwise, it's just on your face."

As the chief of police for Salt Lake City, Chris Burbank provided the face and voice of the department. He regularly appeared on radio programs talking about the latest efforts that police were undertaking to ensure public safety. On one such broadcast, Serio and JJ joined Burbank as guests. They talked about the K9 Squad and the important work that the highly trained dogs perform for the city. The highlight of the show, of course, was JJ baying.

"I could talk for a week and not get that kind of response," said Burbank. "Although it's certainly not the reason to get a bloodhound program, there is a lot of goodwill that comes from that. He was a natural fit. JJ became the lovable arm of the police department."

SKULL

The skull is long and narrow, with the occipital peak very pronounced. The brows are not prominent, although, owing to the deep-set eyes, they may have that appearance.

January 2004

Serio's third child was his first with two legs. A fiery little girl, Mikaela probably thought it perfectly natural to bobble around two gentle beasts that always greeted her with wet noses and warm tongues. Josie, the social butterfly of the family, followed Mikaela around wherever she went. JJ calculated his encounters with the bambina. He slept most of the day on his doggie bed, but once Mikaela progressed to solid foods, he always drew near at feeding time. JJ and Josie slurped up anything that hit the floor, sometimes inhaled food dangling from her unwary hands, and always "cleaned up" her high chair. The high chair ended up a slobbery mess every time, but dog saliva—even the thick blood-hound variety—is easier to clean up than dried puree of peas.

Serio worked the graveyard shift—now 7 p.m. to 5 a.m.—so he escaped most of Mikaela's middle-of-the-night demands, but he had his turn during the day. He returned from work around 5:30 a.m. and took Mikaela so Lisa could get some sleep. Holding his little girl carefully, he bounced on an exercise ball until she fell back asleep.

As with any new parent, adequate sleep proved elusive. But work was going better than ever. Serio's new K9 sergeant definitely helped. When Jon Richey first took the job, he didn't think much of bloodhounds. Twenty years prior, at the age of nineteen, he broke records as the youngest police officer in the state of Utah. He had been working with German shepherds ever since and won numerous local and national K9 competition titles, as well as two international championships. Richey had seen German shepherds do it all, so he didn't see much need for a bloodhound.

He tagged along with Serio during training sessions. For Serio training was always a test. He felt the pressure to prove the bloodhound program every time. Fortunately, what Richey saw impressed him, but he wasn't convinced until he got his own hands on the leash. One day Serio offered to let Richey handle the line on a track set down for Josie. Richey was used to a German shepherd, methodical, cutting back and forth, acknowledging the track, taking time to follow it from end to end.

As Richey described it, "He handed me Josie, and she took the scent and just took off like a rocket. It was all I could do to hang onto her leash. She was on the track just exactly as it was laid, but I felt absolutely useless to the dog. Whereas with a German shepherd, I felt like I needed to help the dog reacquire the track when it was lost and play a big part in the running of the track. When I handled Josie, she didn't let me influence her with the leash. She knew exactly what she was doing. That's the day I became sold on the bloodhound."

Richey also noticed the sharp division between his four German shepherd handlers and his one bloodhound handler. "Mike pretty much did his own thing," Richey said. "He had to find his own resources and wasn't really integrated into the squad." A fan of statistics, Richey devised a weighted scale to measure the productivity of his K9 teams. A misdemeanor arrest earned three points, and a felony arrest earned seven points. The scale was the same for all the dog teams, but patrol dog teams are multidisciplinary, so they had more opportunities to accumulate points. The German shepherds could earn points for drug detection (three points for marijuana, seven points for cocaine), tactical deployments apprehending a suspect in a known location, and tracking. As a single-purpose dog, JJ could only earn points for tracking. Nevertheless, when Richey crunched the numbers, he discovered that Serio and JJ's productivity consistently outstripped the rest of the squad *combined*. "That opened my eyes wide."

The other handlers saw Serio as the competition. Richey wanted to work that friction to his advantage while also integrating Serio more fully into the squad. The patrol dog handlers trained more and more in the tracking arena because they didn't want a bloodhound to outdo their shepherds. But Serio and JJ kept getting better. Richey abolished the policy that sometimes restricted Serio from deploying JJ on aggravated cases involving a weapon. Instead, whenever possible, he had the bloodhound and patrol dogs work in tandem. Serio and JJ handled the track, followed by a patrol dog team in the event that, when found, the suspect became aggressive or fled. The German shepherd could then "resolve the situation" if necessary. JJ and the German shepherds had worked together before but not in such a practiced or coordinated manner. The new K9 team effort soon paid dividends.

• • •

Patricia Watkins, twenty-one years old, applied to the Alameda County Sheriff's Office in the Bay Area to impose a restraining order on her boyfriend, Donald Lacy, but she didn't show up for the hearing, so the sheriff's office didn't issue the order. It wouldn't have helped anyway. On March 6 she drove to her mother's house and dropped off her daughter for the night. When she got back in the car with her two-year-old son, Lacy was hiding in the backseat. He threatened her and told her to drive. Lacy wanted his family back. He was the little boy's father, and Patricia was pregnant with his child. They stayed the night at a motel in Oakland, the first of three nights of terror and abuse.

The next day they drove to Reno, Nevada, and stayed at a hotel. The violence escalated. Lacy burned her legs with cigarettes, strangled her to near unconsciousness, punched her in the face, severely lacerating her upper lip, and raped her. The abuse continued in the car the next day. Lacy was taking Patricia and the boy to his uncle's house in Minnesota.

But Lacy lost control of the car and spun out, landing in sagebrush in a small ditch by the freeway. Two cars stopped to help, but the car hadn't sustained any noticeable damage, so Lacy drove on. A little while later, the left front tire blew out. He got out and changed the tire. While he was doing so, three Nevada state troopers returning from their workstation stopped at the scene to assist. An additional trooper who'd seen the car pulling away from where they'd spun off the road also stopped. Lacy paced back and forth and wouldn't come within five feet of the troopers. Patricia remained in the car with her son.

"Why are you acting so nervous?" one of the troopers asked, point blank.

"I don't have my driver's license," Lacy said. "My license is suspended, and I don't know what will happen to me."

When asked his name, Lacy gave his brother's name, Mario Worthy, but provided his own birth date and social security number. He probably didn't want to use his own name because he had an outstanding warrant for a probation violation for "corporal injury on spouse cohabitant." Another trooper asked Patricia for her information. He observed her bandaged lip, but she gave no indication that she was in any danger.

After both sets of information from Lacy and Patricia came back with suspended licenses, the troopers told Lacy to drive into Elko, the nearest town, and park the vehicle until they could locate a licensed driver. Lacy exited the freeway into Elko because he thought the troopers were watching—but he didn't stop.

Later that day Patricia's mother contacted the Alameda County Sheriff's Office to report that her daughter and grandson were missing. In addition to reporting a missing person, the Alameda Sheriff's Office issued an Amber Alert for Patricia's two-year-old boy.

Sometime after crossing into Utah, Patricia's lip split open again. It was bleeding badly, and she convinced Lacy to take her to the hospital. Near midnight they stopped at the Mountain West Medical Center in Tooele. Lacy stayed close to Patricia the entire time they were at the hospital. The emergency room staff cleaned and rebandaged Patricia's lip and, due to the severity of the injury, directed her to contact a cosmetic surgeon at LDS Hospital in Salt Lake City, about thirty miles away. The medical staff provided Lacy and Patricia with printed directions to the hospital. When filling out the conditions of admission and consent to medical treatment form, Patricia wrote "Please help" in the box next to her name. The nurse who treated her saw "Please help" on the form but misinterpreted it as a request for financial assistance regarding the medical bills and didn't say anything about it.

Half an hour later, Patricia checked into the emergency room at LDS Hospital in Salt Lake. She had her son with her, but Lacy was asked to wait outside. He didn't want to leave Patricia's side. A nurse contacted Cameron Platt, a police officer working security in the emergency room. She indicated that a female patient with a young child had been the victim of a domestic assault. Officer Platt called for additional officers. Platt told Lacy that he wasn't allowed in the room, which visibly upset the man. While waiting for the additional officers to arrive, Platt spoke with Patricia, and she gave him a brief account of being kidnapped in California three days before. Platt returned to the waiting area as Officers Randy Bushman and Michael Black-burn arrived.

"What's your name?" Platt asked Lacy.

"Mario," Donald Lacy said.

Platt took hold of Lacy's left arm. The man pulled away and fled toward the exit doors. The officers gave chase. Platt tried to pin Lacy against the doors, but their breakaway hinges opened outward. The force of the two men caused the doors to slam out against the stops and recoil inward. The left door struck Platt on the side of the head, and he lost hold of Lacy. All three officers continued their pursuit on foot but lost sight of Lacy within a few seconds as he rounded the corner to the east and disap-peared from view.

Platt called for a Plan C, a containment, from 6th Avenue to 8th Avenue and from E Street to F Street. Four officers in patrol cars arrived rapidly at the designated corners, setting up a perimeter, and turned on their lights. A containment boxes in a suspect so other officers arriving at the scene can focus their search within the block. If the suspect breaks the containment, and the officer who has a direct line of sight isn't picking his nose, he'll see the guy cross. If he does, the containment moves over, setting up a new box.

Serio had heard dispatch call out an Amber Alert suspect who had fled on foot. He and JJ arrived at the hospital and got the last known location from Officer Platt. Even though he didn't have a scent article, JJ picked up a track right away. Dog han-dlers call it the "fear scent," the adrenaline-charged scent trail left by a fleeing suspect. It's hard to replicate in training, but JJ had encountered it plenty of times and bayed loudly when his nose hit it. Half a block farther east, still within the contain-ment zone, JJ tracked to a garage, his head popped up, and he pranced back and forth, baying skyward, desperately searching all around. After a minute or two with no luck, Serio suspected that the suspect had hid in the garage, then fled again. Not completely confident, however, he called over his K9 sergeant, who was at the scene with his young German shepherd, Oscar.

"Hey, Jon, JJ is really hot in this garage. Bring Oscar up here, and double-check it."

As soon as Richey headed his way, Serio pulled JJ out of the garage in hopes that he could find an exit trail away from the scent pool in the garage. Once JJ got to the east side of the garage, he started searching the front lawn of the adjacent property.

"What's going on, what's going on?" said a woman coming out of the house, concerned with all the commotion at 1:00 a.m.

"We're looking for someone who ran from the police," Serio said. "Please, get back in the house."

During the brief interchange, JJ's nostrils bounced along the ground. Before Serio could see if the woman went back inside, JJ bayed and pulled him off to the races again.

K9 Officer Cale Lennberg had arrived at the scene with his German shepherd, Elvis. Richey directed him to stay loosely in the area of Serio and JJ. Lennberg deployed Elvis on 8th Avenue and tried to stay one block north. Serio was easy to follow; JJ was baying eastbound. As JJ's baying increased in intensity, Lennberg knew that the bloodhound was getting close to the suspect. Running quickly, he and Elvis got behind Serio and JJ, ready to resolve any kind of situation that came up.

The small entourage arrived at the intersection of 7th Avenue and F Street, at the edge of the police containment. JJ cut across the street and continued eastbound through a yard and to a T-intersection in an alley between houses. JJ turned left and quickly stopped short. Serio could see that he'd made the wrong turn and pulled him back. Elvis, a few feet behind, lifted his tail and head and began sniffing the air intensely. German shepherds are exceptionally good at air scenting. Elvis had picked up the scent trail, and it went right. Both German shepherd and bloodhound ran down the alley as fast as they could pull their handlers and stopped at a large pine tree. JJ bayed and Elvis barked, both dogs indicating a high alert. The suspect was right there. Serio and Lennberg lit up the thirty-foot tree with their flashlights.

"We got him," Lennberg called on the radio.

Donald Lacy clung to the tree, twenty feet up. The officers called him down. "All right, all right," Lacy said. "I'm coming." He started to climb down slowly, but his head was scanning in different directions.

Richey, who had arrived with Oscar and more officers, looked up. "I don't think he's going to cooperate."

The other officers agreed. "He's going to Peter Pan his way out of the tree," said one, coining a term used again and again to describe a nimble criminal soaring above the ground.

They yelled for him not to try it, but about fifteen feet off the ground, Donald jumped to the end of a tree branch, hung down, swung his body, and dropped onto the roof of a house. Lennberg and Richey ran around to the other side of the house, ready to release Elvis and Oscar if the suspect hit the ground. JJ's work was done, but Serio's wasn't. "Here," he said to Officer Bushman, handing him JJ's leash, "I'm going up after him."

In college Serio ran his own business, Mike's Gutter and Window Cleaning Service. For big jobs he persuaded his college roommate to help out. Possessing a healthy fear of heights, his roommate stayed on the ladder, holding on with one hand while scooping out gutter muck with the other. Serio, however, squatted on the edge of the pitched roof, sometimes three stories up, and reached down with both hands to do the job.

Serio got on the roof—but the suspect was nowhere to be seen. Serio climbed down on the other side into a narrow alley, and he heard Lennberg yell, "I'm gonna send the dog!" Serio next saw the suspect's head pop over the top of the seven-foot-tall wooden fence right in front of him. Two feet away, Serio drew his gun and pointed it at him.

"Police! Get down!"

Lacy's eyes grew wide, and he stopped for an instant, but Serio could tell he wasn't going to comply. Lacy continued to climb.

"Dammit," Serio said, holstering his gun and climbing up after him. From the roof of a garage, Lacy jumped to an adjoining roof, then to another. On the last roof, pitched at a moderate angle on both sides, Serio spotted the suspect sprawled out flat. "Don't move!" he yelled, still on the move himself. "Let me see your hands!" Lacy got up to run again, immediately tackled back to the shingled roof. Serio got him in a head and arm lock and tried to get the man's other hand behind his back to handcuff him, but the suspect still wouldn't comply. Serio pressed him into the roof. "We're going to do whatever it takes to get you into custody."

Lacy finally turned his head and looked at Serio, ready to give in. "Whatever you do," he said, "do *not* let that dog get me." Officer Blackburn climbed onto the roof and helped Serio get him handcuffed.

"I've never heard anything like that in my life," Lacy continued, before they lowered him from the roof to officers on the ground. "That was a dog, right?"

Serio had heard it before. Captured criminals often told Serio that JJ's baying terrified them as they were fleeing and haunted them when they went into hiding and heard the noise getting closer. Cynophobia is the abnormal fear of dogs, but that's not what these guys had. They feared the unknown. Some had it more than others. One suspect, who had robbed a 7-Eleven and hid in a shed where JJ found him, literally shit his pants. The arresting officer had to put sheets down in the back of his patrol car before he took the guy to jail.

Donald Lacy was charged with aggravated kidnapping, child kidnapping, two counts of rape, two counts of class A assault, assault in the presence of a child, reckless child endangerment, and resisting arrest. Five months later he accepted a plea bargain that ended his trial shortly after it began. In Utah the sentence for a first-degree felony calls for five years to life in prison. Charged with four first-degree felonies, he initially faced a minimum jail sentence of twenty years, but Lacy pleaded guilty to the lesser charge of attempted kidnapping, a third-degree felony with a maximum sentence of five years in jail.

NECK, SHOULDERS, AND CHEST

The neck is long, the shoulders muscular and well sloped backwards; the ribs are well sprung; and the chest well let down between the forelegs, forming a deep keel.

May 2004

The police can respond to a crime scene as fast as a 6.0-liter V8 engine can travel, but institutional change across the thin blue line happens at a crawl. For five years JJ had served as the lone police bloodhound in Utah. It was time for some company.

Serio and JJ unarguably had made a positive impact. Their training ties with Multi-Agency K9 also helped to spread the bloodhound word to other parts of the Salt Lake Valley. The South Jordan Police Department followed suit first. With a population of just over fifty thousand, South Jordan lies eighteen miles south of Salt Lake City, largely a commuter town. The crime rate is significantly lower than in the capital city, but enough criminals get up to no good to warrant South Jordan's own dedicated K9 Squad.

Allen Crist had worked for South Jordan with a Labrador retriever trained in narcotics detection, but he didn't know much about bloodhounds. His assistant chief heard good things about Serio and JJ and told Crist, if he was interested, to look into it. Crist called Serio and soon was witnessing it firsthand, running behind the duo. He was sold on the bloodhound, but dogs don't come cheap, particularly to small departments with limited resources. Crist's research turned up a private dog breeder in Bluffdale, Utah, only six miles away. When Crist called Bitterroot Bloodhounds and explained about adding a bloodhound to their K9 Squad, Bitterroot agreed to donate one and gave Crist the pick of the next litter.

Crist and Serio stood among eighteen wrinkly bloodhound puppies with enough energy to power a small town. All around ten weeks old, they came from two different litters. Serio had experience selecting a bloodhound, so Crist had asked him to come along to help. But how do you test for potential tracking greatness? Serio took the obvious shortcut and looked for traits that best matched JJ as a puppy.

The two officers rounded up all eighteen puppies, which is much easier to do than with cats, and put them together in a group. Then they stepped away and watched. The puppies that stayed in the group the longest, wanting to be with their brothers and sisters, were ruled out. Serio was looking for the puppies that wanted to explore. Is the puppy independent? Curious? Does it want to discover the outside world? Does it have the drive? Crist and Serio played with the puppies, then ran away. They looked for the ones that wanted to find them to play some more. They narrowed it down to a clear two and made a tough choice for the final one.

Wyatt started training at three months old. Crist rolled a piece of meat across the floor, hid it around the corner, and Wyatt tracked right to it. Wyatt got an early start to his career. "He had his first find at eight months old," Crist said. "He could barely walk without tripping over his own ears, but he tracked down two guys who fled from the Sandy Police Department in a stolen vehicle and crashed in South Jordan."

Since Serio and JJ had already shown many of the Salt Lake Valley's patrol officers and K9 handlers what a bloodhound team could do, Crist didn't face the same institutional contention. JJ had converted a lot of unbelievers and fence riders. What Crist did have to navigate, however, was an extremely high bar. Were Crist and Wyatt as good? Could Serio and JJ's success be replicated? Serio did what he could to quell the questions. The two men trained their bloodhounds together, but they didn't often overlap on actual deployments. The territory they covered lay far apart, one on the north end and the other on the south end of the valley.

Once, however, they met in the middle, both responding to a call in West Valley where an armed robbery suspect had fled from the police. "Clearly Mike and JJ would have been the better choice because they had the experience," Crist said. "But Mike stepped aside and allowed me to deploy Wyatt." Serio kept JJ in the truck and ran behind them. Wyatt tracked the armed robbery suspect down, getting credit for an excellent felony apprehension. Another department in the valley getting their own bloodhound and having success proved that Serio's experiment was more than a one-hit wonder.

• • •

Josie never had trouble sleeping, but now she could relax even more. Serio's other bloodhound—Lisa's baby—had been trained and brought out on a few cases, but she preferred life outside work. Josie seemed happiest when at home sleeping or hitched to a sled alongside JJ as Mikaela's personal reindeer, pulling the bundled-up, laughing toddler. With another police bloodhound in the Salt Lake Valley, some of the replacement pressure eased off Josie. A temporary substitute position was one thing, but full-time work was for other dogs.

Wyatt was nabbing suspects on the south side of the valley, and JJ was getting them everywhere else. In November 2004 the Metro Gang Squad received a tip from an informant, and officers were following a car driven by Troy Mayne. The current list of crimes for which he had not served time, including a particularly aggravated robbery, put him at the top of the list: Troy Mayne was Utah's Most Wanted Criminal.

At 9:18 p.m. Troy was pulled over for a traffic stop near the Tesoro gas station on 2100 South 500 East. He ran. In a Plan C

The Salt Lake City K9 Squad logo
Image courtesy of Salt Lake City Police Department

Mikaela thought JJ and Josie were her personal reindeer, when they pulled her laughing through the snow on a sled.

Photograph courtesy of Mike and Lisa Serio

NECK, SHOULDERS, AND CHEST

containment, officers searched the area. The vehicle had been spotted in South Salt Lake's jurisdiction, but it was stopped in Salt Lake City. The officers wondered who was in charge, but everybody wanted to catch this guy, so they called in a Utah Highway Patrol helicopter.

Serio had been patrolling the area when he heard the triple beep and the magic words for a K9 handler: "Suspect fled on foot." JJ picked up the track near the abandoned car and brought Serio north to a wooden fence, where they found a hunting knife with a folding blade. JJ put his front paws up on the fence and bayed. He wanted over. Serio grabbed his hind legs, tossed him, and quickly jumped the fence after him. JJ hooked into the track and immediately pulled. Serio called on the radio, reporting their location and direction.

Across the street, they cut between houses, over two more fences and through yards, before popping out on Ramona Avenue. The Metro Gang officers had been shadowing their position, running parallel along 500 East Street, and Serio caught a glimpse of them about sixty yards to his left. Then he spotted a television news van. A man had exited the van and was running toward him, a video camera over his shoulder and a bright light shining right in Serio's face. The news stations monitored the police channels, particularly at night, and showed up to potentially newsworthy events. Utah's Most Wanted on the run, a UHP helicopter flying overhead, and police officers swarming the scene—this one definitely had potential. Serio usually didn't mind the media's presence, but the camera light was shining right at them, and the aggressive presence was distracting JJ.

"Can you please get out of here?" Serio asked. "I'm trying to work my dog."

Sometimes, the media ignored him, exercising their right to be where they pleased. This time, however, after leaving the light on for a few more seconds, the cameraman got back in the van and pulled away.

JJ lost the track at Ramona Avenue. Serio kept casting him, in the hopes of reacquiring the scent trail, but he had to call his sergeant and tell him JJ lost it. "You're welcome to deploy your dogs," Serio said. Richey and Oscar, along with another K9 team from his squad, started a yard-to-yard search with their German shepherds in the area. Serio and JJ moved farther north to continue the search. By this point Officer David Wierman had joined Serio and followed as backup. About forty-five minutes later, with no leads, officers who had come to help began to leave. For a time, the scene was booming, but that changed shortly after JJ lost the track. The helicopter had flown away, and the media disappeared. The watch commander called off the containment and everyone left—everyone except Serio, JJ, Wierman, and Utah's Most Wanted criminal, that is.

Serio kept working JJ, searching the neighborhood high and low. Wierman, friends with Serio since their rookie days, ran behind the bloodhound team any chance he could. "It was just fun," he said. Listening to JJ bay and lead to a hiding criminal was better than any movie, but watching Serio and JJ go for a walk for well over an hour in the middle of the cold November night, however, was duller than a middle school botany film.

"Dude," Wierman said, "let's walk over to the 7-Eleven and get a drink."

"No," Serio said, "I'm still going to check around. I want to go back to where I absolutely know JJ had the track."

"All right," Wierman said, a little weary, but he stuck with him. Serio had experienced plenty of times when even his backup officer had thrown in the towel, leaving him and JJ to search alone, often in vain, but once in a blue moon . . .

When JJ got back to just before Ramona Avenue, he seemed to pick up a track heading east. Working slowly and methodically, he moved along, his body language stronger at each step of the way. It had been a few hours, so it probably took JJ a little while to remember the original scent. A few yards farther east, he found it, baying and pulling Serio around the corner of an apartment building. Holding onto the leash fifteen feet behind his dog, Serio turned the corner and saw JJ standing on top of a man hiding behind a large air-conditioning compressor.

Wierman did the honors, and Serio called it in. Metro Gang officers arrived first, but the media came right behind them. Troy Mayne's capture meant some other lucky fellow got a promotion that night to Utah's Most Wanted.

"Everybody knows who JJ is," Serio said, speaking on camera to the KSL News reporter. "They don't know me, but they know who he is."

"I know the dog gets a lot of the credit," Wierman said, "but Mike is pretty tenacious. Where many people would pull the plug, Mike just keeps going. He's the Energizer bunny."

LEGS AND FEET

The forelegs are straight and large in bone, with elbows squarely set; the feet strong and well knuckled up; the thighs and second thighs (gaskins) are very muscular; the hocks well bent and let down and squarely set.

March 2006

Some years are busier than others. For Serio and JJ 2006 was just such a year. Either everything was happening at once, or, if one significant event ran its course, a new one grabbed the baton and took off without a pause for breath.

One evening in late March 2006, Angie McDougall was washing dishes after dinner when she realized her three-year-old son, Brandon, was missing. Thinking he was around the house somewhere, she had the rest of her kids help look for him. They couldn't find him, so they expanded the search to the school behind their house. With still no sign and panic rising, Angie asked neighbors to join in the search. Soon the whole neighborhood was out looking and knocking on doors. About an hour had passed since Angie first noticed that Brandon was missing. She called the police.

Because nightfall was approaching and the temperature was expected to dip below freezing, Dave Askerlund, supervising officer on the scene, called for all available motors on his squad and asked for anyone else who was free. Amid the many police cars and flashing lights, a lot of people were looking for Brandon. Serio had just left his house, heading to work to start his graveyard shift. He flipped on his radio and heard officers talking back and forth about a missing child.

"This is Kilo 855. I'm en route up there. If you can, try to limit foot traffic." He made the request out of habit. Scores of people had already been combing the area for over an hour. The scent contamination would make it harder for JJ to pick up the boy's smell. Serio pulled up to the house as close as he could, with all the police vehicles parked haphazardly about. He knew that, with the time lapse and contamination, JJ's chances were minimal. Someone gave him pairs of Brandon's socks and shoes that the three-year-old had worn recently.

In front of the house, with the socks and shoes on the ground next to JJ, Serio put the harness on him and asked the question. "Are you ready to go to *work?*"

JJ bayed, sniffed the shoes, and began. Serio cast JJ, who hooked into a track going north. Just two doors down from where they started, JJ walked up the front steps of a house, let out a bay, and poked his nose beneath a porch bench. His tail was wagging. A little boy was hiding underneath the bench. The many police cars and officers had scared Brandon, who hid until he hoped his mother would find him.

"I can't remember a situation where so many compliments were given to the department and officers on scene," said Askerlund. It was one of the shortest tracks of his career, but for JJ it offered a welcome change to get a big hug from the person he found instead of being called "that damned dog!"

• • •

JJ wasn't the only bloodhound in the valley making headlines, though. Wyatt was doing great work with Allen Crist, catching fugitives in double-digit numbers for the South Jordan PD. A year after he started, South Salt Lake also followed suit, partnering K9 Officer Alan Hunsaker with a bloodhound named Max. The valley now had three police bloodhounds.

Serio and JJ maintained close ties with the other bloodhound teams, and they all trained together when they could. Salt Lake had a crime rate totaling more than five times that of South Salt Lake and South Jordan combined, so JJ didn't have much free

JJ and 3-year-old Brandon Crowley, whom JJ happily found just a few houses away

*Photograph courtesy of Laura Lamando/*Salt Lake Tribune

time. Patrol officers used to having a bloodhound find their suspects on the run noticed when he wasn't on duty or available to respond. Even more pressing, however, was JJ's age. He was still strong and healthy, but at nine years old he had already exceeded the average retirement age of police dogs. Salt Lake City needed another bloodhound.

You might think that departmental approval for another bloodhound to work alongside and eventually replace JJ would be an easy call. It wasn't. Fortunately, this time around, Serio had a few more allies.

Sergeant Jon Richey had been knocking on doors for two years, throwing his K9 productivity statistics around and making the case for another bloodhound. He reiterated that the bloodhound would in no way replace a patrol dog but rather complement them. "They're like the sniper on a SWAT team," said Richey. "He's not the entire team, but he's an important part of it. For looking, a bloodhound is the best tool for the job." Richey was rebuffed every time, but no doubt he loosened the lid a little.

Lieutenant Melody Gray, recently appointed commander over the K9 Squad, was listening. By her own admission she wasn't a sympathetic ear to the bloodhound cause when Serio first started with JJ. "Mike fought really hard, and I was very skeptical," Lieutenant Gray said. "My dad was a K9 handler, and I grew up with these dogs, the shepherds. I was one of those who said the shepherds can do it all; you don't need bloodhounds." But time and the preponderance of the evidence changed her opinion. Lieutenant Gray also listened to her officers.

When the idea for adding a second bloodhound to the Salt Lake City K9 Squad made its way up the chain of command, some of the pushback cited it as a waste of personnel. Assigning another bloodhound handler meant taking another patrol officer off the street. Others thought the opposite: adding a bloodhound meant getting an *extra* officer. K9 officers also helped handle non-dog-related calls. Gray put together a survey and sent it out to all the patrol officers. She knew the decision would most affect the patrol officers, and they could best evaluate the usefulness of a bloodhound on the street.

Eighty-three percent of all patrol officers reported working on a call with a bloodhound. One hundred percent of those officers said the bloodhound's involvement was beneficial. Seventy-seven percent of all patrol officers had requested a bloodhound team when one was not available, and 94 percent said they would recommend an additional bloodhound team to maintain seven-day-a-week bloodhound coverage. When asked why or why not, the answers varied in their details, but the support for more bloodhounds came loud and clear:

- "JJ has caught more bad guys than most officers put together. You only have to listen to the radio when JJ and Officer Serio are working to know how valuable they are."

- "Man-hours are saved when the bloodhound quickly tracks a bandit. I have *never* heard an officer complain when the bloodhound is available, but I have heard the opposite."

- "Patrol has already been defeated when the bloodhound deploys. My personal experience is that, when the hound hits the street, we catch the bad guy at about a 90 percent clip."

- "JJ's success rate is very high. When he works along with a shepherd, they are unstoppable."

- "The bloodhound program speaks for itself. It's too bad not everyone is listening."

The list went on.

Lieutenant Gray's survey drummed up a lot of talk. While officers on the street overwhelmingly supported another bloodhound, some of the brass in key positions remained adamantly opposed to the idea. After compiling the survey responses, Gray and Richey put together a proposal to send to the deputy chief. Meanwhile, Lieutenant Craig Gleason was also fighting for the bloodhound program on behalf of his patrol officers.

As one of Serio's graveyard shift sergeants, Gleason had supported the bloodhound program early on and played a role in securing their initial trial run. The first time he was on a patrol call with JJ, however, he wasn't so helpful. JJ had been deployed to look for a homicide suspect. He picked up a track at the scene of the shooting, ran directly across the street, and alerted on a house. Gleason told Serio that his dog was mistaken. "My feeling at the time," said Gleason, "was what kind of knucklehead would shoot his neighbor, then go hide in his house directly across the street?" A rookie cop with a new bloodhound, Serio listened and pulled JJ off. "Later we were informed that that was exactly where he was," said Gleason. "I talked them out of a capture."

If the first time seeing JJ at work didn't convince Gleason, another one did. Gleason showed up to a crime scene, blocks away from where Serio and JJ had already started tracking a suspect. He got out of his car to look around. A guy on foot ran toward the back end of a cheap hotel, reeking of *eau de crook*.

"Don't move," said Gleason.

"Well, I was just—"

"No, sit down." Gleason could hear JJ baying blocks away but getting closer. "Did you just happen to rob a store back there?"

"No," the guy said, "that wasn't me."

"Do you hear that dog?" asked Gleason.

"Yeah."

"Well, I'm betting in, like, three minutes that dog is gonna run right into you."

Sure enough, a few minutes later, JJ came into view pulling Serio behind him, ran up, and bayed right in the guy's face.

Gleason staunchly supported them ever since and regularly wrote e-mails to Serio's superiors detailing recent deployments that led to otherwise unlikely captures. When the push to add another bloodhound came up, Gleason advocated the cause to superiors positioned between him and the chief. The brass argued that Serio had had his chance with the bloodhound program and hadn't produced the statistics necessary to justify additional funding. Gleason counterargued that they weren't being fair in citing Serio's batting average for arrests as not significantly better than the patrolmen's averages.

"The fact is," said Gleason, "in almost every case we'd already struck out. I've only been on one bloodhound deployment and thought, *Yeah, I would have caught that guy.* In almost every case where he catches the guy, it's like three blocks down that way, six hundred yards that way, down the alley, and behind the dumpster. Everyone he catches, the guy would have walked."

Gleason tried to figure out why they were resisting and remembered a conversation he'd had with a German shepherd handler who bristled when Gleason brought up bloodhounds' amazing capabilities. The handler insisted that his dog could do anything a bloodhound could do and more. "It was like you were talking to somebody about race or where they were from," said Gleason. "When somebody has an emotional response like that, they will construct facts to support how they feel."

The bloodhound issue went before the sergeants on the graveyard shift. They learned that, even to consider adding another bloodhound, they had to give up one of their patrol officers to staff the handler position. With tight resources various shifts and squads were always competing with one another for positions. Everyone felt understaffed. Some predicted that all the sergeants would say, "No, don't touch my people." The response surprised a lot of people. They all agreed: "We'll take the bloodhound."

Somewhere along the way, Lieutenant Gray's proposal made it to the chief's desk. Whatever the deciding factors may have been, the end result mattered. The chief approved a new bloodhound and handler position. Officer Randy Hunnewell and Moe soon joined the Salt Lake City K9 Squad.

• • •

Expectations for JJ ran high, making any missteps or failed deployments all the more notable. JJ had made seemingly impossible finds on numerous occasions, so he was called out more frequently to help on all sorts of cases with a low probability of finding anything: The burglar likely had fled hours ago; the missing child had probably been picked up in a car near the last sighting; neighbors and other officers and dogs had already crisscrossed the area, severely contaminating the scent trail. Many handlers only deployed their dogs on high-probability cases. Serio believed so strongly in JJ's tracking abilities that he deployed the bloodhound in just about any situation where there was someone to find. It brought his successful apprehension rate down, but in the end he caught a lot more people. Serio didn't care about his batting average; he wanted total hits and swung at any chance he got.

In July 2006 a five-year-old girl named Destiny Norton went missing from her Salt Lake City home. Family, friends, and neighbors combed the area looking for any sign of where she might have gone or been taken. More than six hours later, the police were called. The lieutenant on duty that night was C. T. Smith, Serio's former K9 sergeant. He immediately got the K9 handlers and their dogs on the scene. It was Serio's day off, so he wasn't one of them. The K9 teams worked with what they had, but they didn't have a chance of finding anything. Serio and JJ wouldn't have had a chance, either. Dozens of people contaminated the search area, a densely populated apartment complex, and too much time had passed. Lieutenant Smith didn't call Serio at home, but maybe he should have—not because Serio and JJ could have helped find the girl but because the public and the media demanded it.

"Where is the bloodhound?" a lot of people asked. The media had reported on JJ's numerous finds, and the family and neighbors of a missing five-year-old had seen on the news or read in the paper about the bloodhound who "always gets his man." Feeling the pressure build, the department called Serio and told him to bring JJ.

Eighteen hours after Destiny Norton was reported missing, Serio, JJ, and Josie arrived at the scene. The temperature had reached 102 degrees. The dogs wouldn't last long. He brought Josie along so she could work when JJ got tired out. Serio was hoping for a miracle, but he knew it was largely futile. They did their best. JJ didn't know what he was supposed to follow—there was no scent trail to find. He wandered around for an hour and half, drooping in the heat. Serio put JJ in his air-conditioned truck, got Josie out, and repeated the task. Later that day Chief Burbank was addressing the community when a reporter asked, "What did the bloodhound say?"

Serio knew that he was there with his bloodhounds to show that the police were doing everything they could to find Destiny. The knowledge didn't lessen the pressure. The majority of the public and even a lot of the people in his own department didn't understand a bloodhound's capabilities. The embellished accounts of many dog handlers, civilian and police, didn't help matters, but Serio felt his own success with JJ contributed to the misunderstanding. People read about Officer Serio and JJ tracking down two robbery suspects nine blocks going left, right, over fences, through alleys, and locating them inside a trailer. If a bloodhound can do that, surely it should be able to find someone within even just a couple of blocks.

"They don't understand what a dog has to sort through," Serio said. "You've got to have certain things in place: The contamination has got to be low, the time lapse has to be reasonable, the vegetation helps, all those things, kind of like stars in a row for things to be in your favor. They think we're CSI, and we're not."

After an eight-day search, the police found Destiny's body in her killer's basement, a neighbor who lived fewer than a hundred feet away. Craig Gregerson had lured Destiny into his house. When she began to scream, he put his hand over her mouth until her body went limp. She died before the search even began.

Scent dogs pick up a track and follow it. The longer they follow, the more confident they become. JJ and the other dogs that searched for Destiny faced an impossible situation. Her scent was all over the place, so there was no track to be found. But the size of the odds never diminishes the stigma or the tragedy of a failed track.

EYES

The eyes are deeply sunk in the orbits, the lids assuming a lozenge or diamond shape, in consequence of the lower lids being dragged down and averted by the heavy flews. The eyes correspond with the general tone of color of the animal, varying from deep hazel to yellow. The hazel color is, however, to be preferred.

August 2006

JJ was looking for a man who had tried to hit two policemen with his truck and shot at another with a sawed-off shotgun. Taylorsville police officers on the southwestern side of Salt Lake City had received a tip from a neighbor reporting suspected drug activity and stolen vehicles. After confirming that at least one vehicle was stolen, police set up surveillance on the house.

Criminals receive tips, too, though. A friend of the suspect appears to have called on a cell phone after spotting the surveillance. Around 1:00 a.m. Christopher Mower, a convicted felon with a smattering of drug, assault, and weapons violation charges, accelerated his red 1994 Chevy Silverado truck out of the driveway. Officer Brett Miller turned on his flashing lights and positioned his patrol car in front of the truck's path. Instead of slowing down, Mower swerved toward the patrol car. Officer Miller swiftly maneuvered out of the way to avoid a head-on collision. The pursuit had begun.

Officer Bryan Marshall was driving southbound toward the pursuit. Seeing the suspect's vehicle coming his way, he got in the left turn lane to hold the intersection. Mower crossed three lanes and drove right for Officer Marshall, who turned sharply to get out of the way. Driving behind the vehicle as it fled into a neighborhood through a series of turns, Officer Joseph Corbett saw the driver's arm extend a long object toward him. The gun fired and struck Corbett's right front bumper. Mower crashed the truck into a fence at the end of a driveway, got out, and ran. A containment perimeter was set up, and K9 units were called to assist.

Word that a police officer had been shot at travels quickly. Police officers from multiple departments arrived to assist. Along with two heavily armed SWAT officers, K9 Officer Christopher

Walden and his German shepherd, Kaiser, ran behind Serio and JJ. Starting at the still running abandoned truck, JJ picked up a track heading east and turned south. They ran into multiple fences, many topped with barbed wire, but one of the officers fortunately had fence cutters so JJ kept as direct a line on the track as possible. JJ found Mower in a detached garage, hiding inside a vehicle.

Arrested suspects run the gamut from sullenly quiet to violently obstreperous. As Officer Scott Miller transported him to the Taylorsville Police Department, Mower was chatty. Concerned now with the health and well-being of all involved, he inquired if everyone was okay.

"I did a stupid thing," said Mower.

"I don't disagree," Miller said flatly.

"Drugs are bad and make people do stupid things." Mower, twenty-two years old, was charged with attempted homicide, aggravated assault on a police officer, theft, felony fleeing, possession of a weapon by a restricted person, and burglary.

• • •

The judicial system relies on a quantitative system to administer punishment. The higher the degree of the crime, the more time served. Qualitatively, however, the system often breaks down. Not all criminals serving the same amount of time are equal. Some are more sinister than others.

Among many other dubious talents, David George Garnett excelled at being a con artist. He went door to door pretending to be a police officer seeking donations for the drug abuse prevention program, DARE. He also posed as a bail bondsman and offered a twenty-two-year-old woman help in getting an acquaintance out of jail. Garnett gave the woman and a friend a ride, dropping off the friend first. Then he took the woman to a motel, told her she "owed him ten thousand dollars' worth of her body," and repeatedly raped her over the next twenty-four hours, threatening to harm her friend if she resisted. When Garnett went to buy drugs the next day, he took her with him. She escaped out of the car and contacted the police.

The police notified the public with a description of the suspect and his car, a white Mercury Topaz. They had been searching for three days when a call came in from a citizen who spotted Garnett driving the car north on Redwood Road. Police responded, and Officer Robert Zubal located the white Mercury behind an abandoned work trailer near the Rose Park Golf Course.

Serio was mopping the floors at home when the call came in around noon. He put JJ in the police truck and covered the ten miles to the scene pretty quickly. Lieutenant Mike Ross, watch commander on the scene, briefed Serio on what they knew.

"This is the car of the guy we've been looking for. We believe he's been living out of this trailer. We think he took off on foot but don't know where he went."

"Where have you searched so far?" Serio asked. He wanted an idea of the best place to put JJ to find a leaving track and also to double-check where they'd already searched. They had cleared the trailer, and officers were searching the nearby neighborhoods. The suspect was assumed to be armed and dangerous, so Mike Hatch and another officer with a rifle followed as backup.

Serio started JJ on the car seat, and he immediately picked up a strong odor that led behind the trailer and to the bank of the Jordan River. JJ's head popped up and pointed northwest along the river. Serio could tell that he got a big whiff of something in that direction, but he held the hound back for a minute. There were a lot of varmints in the area, and Serio didn't want JJ tracking a raccoon or red fox. JJ expressed interest in that direction, but he didn't take the track. Serio circled him back toward the trailer. JJ sniffed hard, but with so many officers around, Serio couldn't be sure. He took JJ southeast of the trailer, but the dog showed no signs of interest in that direction.

Not having a better option, Serio took JJ back to the riverbank. The dog picked up a track, got a little faster, and faster still. JJ bayed and pulled Serio into the thick brush near the water's edge. By October most of the leaves had fallen, but Serio still couldn't see far through the thick brush. It was hard to maneuver among the vegetation, so Serio's backup officers didn't try, figuring he'd turn back around or pop out somewhere farther along the bank. JJ pulled Serio to the water and darted into the mud on the bank. The guy probably jumped the river somewhere nearby, and Serio was looking for physical signs along the bank. JJ bayed, then stared right down into the murky water, his tail wagging. Serio couldn't figure out what the bloodhound was doing until he saw the whites of a pair of eyes.

His body completely submerged, Garnett was hanging on the bank of the Jordan River right below JJ's nose. Serio drew his gun and shouted, "Let me see your hands!" His backup officers charged right to his side in an instant. They hauled the sodden suspect out of the water, through the brush, and into the open. JJ followed, baying loudly, very proud of what he'd done.

The pair ended a busy 2006 with the help of a citizen hero. A sixty-three-year-old woman was walking into the grocery store when a man grabbed her purse. She was scared for her life, but she held on. The man punched her and lacerated her arm. As he fled, her seventy-five-year-old husband attempted to stop the man but fell and cut his forehead. Cynthia Wozencraft witnessed the assault and bravely ran after the man, following him for a block and losing sight of him only as he turned north on the next street. Cynthia told Serio where she'd lost sight of the robber. JJ picked up the trail from there and found the man hiding in a basement stairwell.

Serio soon noticed that JJ wasn't eating with as much enthusiasm as he normally displayed when presented with anything edible—and many things inedible. He always fed JJ dinner before heading to work, but the hound kept doing something funny with his tongue and had a hard time chewing. Lisa pried open JJ's mouth so Serio could take a look. He hoped to find an abscessed tooth or similar problem.

He discovered a black lump on the roof of JJ's mouth.

PART THREE

LEGENDS AND LIONS

I wish I had a dog's heart instead of this one.
For I have loved you like a dog.

—Greg Brown

BACK AND LOIN

The back and loins are strong, the latter deep and slightly arched.

January 2007

Serio reported to work that night, too worried to focus. He called his K9 sergeant, Chris Ward, and explained the situation. "I'm heading down to the pet ER and having them take a look."

Serio always accompanied JJ on his veterinary visits. Sergeant Ward also came to show his support. Dr. Nathan Cox at the Cottonwood Animal Hospital sedated JJ for the biopsy, explaining that, while they'd have to wait for the biopsy results to be certain, he believed that JJ had malignant oral melanoma. Due to the current spread and aggressive form of the cancer, Dr. Cox estimated that JJ would have to be put down in thirty to sixty days.

Serio had never cried in front of a fellow officer before and certainly not his immediate supervisor, but he broke down completely in the emergency room. JJ had been given a death sentence. Sick with grief, Serio could hardly breathe or speak, but he quickly zipped through denial and anger, the first two stages of grief, and jumped to stage three: bargaining.

The day after hearing that JJ had two months to live, Serio met with Dr. Dennis Law, director of the Cottonwood Animal Hospital. Dr. Law explained that canine melanoma is a fairly common but particularly deadly form of cancer in dogs. It had a high chance of metastasizing from the mouth to other parts of the body, most likely lymph nodes within the head, neck, and lungs. Untreated, dogs deteriorated fast, dying within a month or two. Treated with surgery and radiation, the dog could live for up to five months.

"There's got to be something else we can do to prolong his life," said Serio. "Everything that I ever tried and worked so hard for, JJ has busted his ass to prove it."

Dr. Law knew of an experimental study underway at Colorado State University's College of Veterinary Medicine. They were testing a vaccine to treat oral canine melanoma. Law didn't know if JJ would qualify for the study, but he promised to make inquiries. Colorado State had one of the top veterinary schools in the country, and it was Law's alma mater.

Serio couldn't just wait for JJ to die. While Law looked into the Colorado State program, Serio researched canine cancer treatments and called everyone he knew. Dr. Keith Kerstann, a good friend since high school, had been a groomsman at Serio's wedding. He was also a cancer researcher working at the Centers for Disease Control in Atlanta. When Serio called and desperately asked if he knew of anything that might help JJ, Kerstann told him to take a look at recent studies on human melanoma conducted at the Memorial Sloan-Kettering Cancer Center in New York.

"It never really crossed my mind to enroll pets as research subjects," said Dr. Jedd Wolchok, a medical oncologist and one of the lead investigators in the project to develop a melanoma vaccine at Sloan-Kettering. The project began with a conversation between Wolchok and Dr. Philip Bergman, head of oncology at the Animal Medical Center in New York. "We shared our frustration with trying to treat melanoma," said Wolchok, "him in dogs and me in people."

A xenogeneic vaccine introduces biological material from one species into another. A student at Sloan-Kettering had shown that, by injecting human melanoma cells into mice, their immune response effectively killed the foreign cancer cells while also immunizing themselves against future exposure to melanoma cells of their own. The next step was to try it on dogs.

In many ways dogs are particularly well suited for the study of diseases that also affect humans. Dogs and people, sharing the same environment, share many of the same risks. Cancers such as melanoma that are rarer in people are common in dogs, so it's easy to find subjects for clinical trials. Because a dog's life span is accelerated in comparison to a human's, vaccine efficacy on dogs can be seen quickly, whereas results for humans often don't show up for years. Size also matters. Medical machinery such as MRI and CT scanning equipment built for humans can also be used on dogs.

Bergman and Wolchok tested the vaccine on nine dogs that had developed oral melanomas. With a median survival time of more than a year, the results lasted three times as long as conventional therapies, and some dogs survived much longer than the median.

Serio wanted JJ to get that vaccine. He met with JJ's primary veterinarian, Dr. Kris Muscari, with a pile of paperwork and shared with her all the information he had learned about the experimental study in New York. In one of those moments when the Fates stir up the stars to fall in someone's favor, Serio learned that Muscari and Bergman had attended medical school together. "He's the absolute best," said Muscari of Bergman.

After comparing the latest advances of the melanoma vaccine study at Colorado State and the joint Sloan-Kettering/Animal Medical Center study in New York, Muscari met with Serio and Lisa again. "If distance and money didn't matter, you would go to New York," said Muscari. "But obviously Colorado is closer and more convenient and could be a good option."

Serio and Lisa looked at one another. "New York it is." They were going wherever it took. The estimated cost of participating in the study ranged between ten and fifteen thousand dollars—but the money didn't matter. It was a lot, true, but with good credit they could finance it.

In addition to the initial biopsy on the tumor, the veterinary hospital had also done a biopsy of JJ's lymph nodes to see if the cancer had spread. While waiting on results, Muscari called Bergman to see if JJ could get in the study. Those were the longest five days of Serio's life. After seeing the tumor in JJ's mouth, every day without action was excruciating. When Serio learned that his beloved dog got a spot in the program, he went from emotional wreck to having a purpose. They were headed to New York City.

Serio told his K9 sergeant not to ask for any money from the department. JJ's routine veterinary costs were covered, and, thanks to Judy Dencker, the department also had agreed to pay for an MRI that JJ needed a few years back for a pinched nerve in his back. Serio, however, paid for the majority of JJ's veterinary bills, and he had every intention of paying for the extensive treatments in New York, which included five separate trips: one for the initial surgery to remove as much of the tumor as possible along with radiation therapy and four additional trips. The canine melanoma vaccine was still experimental, so it couldn't leave the Animal Medical Center in New York. JJ had to return to the Big Apple once every other week for four vaccinations. Booster vaccinations every six months afterward would follow.

"I don't care if Serio wants to pay for it or not," said Lieutenant Melody Gray when she found out about the costs. On the day Serio and JJ left for New York, Gray arranged for the media to be at the airport. They wanted to interview Serio, but he said no. He was normally happy to talk to the press but not then. They asked if they could still run a story, and at Gray's urging Serio let them take pictures of JJ. Gray and Ward explained to the media that, unlike other dogs in the department, owned by the city, JJ was a contract worker. Serio hired his bloodhound out for his services to the Salt Lake City Police Department. Ward made sure to let the media know that the estimated treatment costs exceeded thirteen thousand dollars, well beyond the department's budget for veterinary care. He made it clear that Serio was going through with the treatments, regardless, but those wishing to make a donation to help defray JJ's medical costs could contact the police department.

Serio was in no condition to talk to the media, but he was glad for his escorts. Along with Lisa and Lieutenant Gray, all the K9 handlers from his squad came to see him and JJ off. But there was a problem. As the lone civilian in the group, airport security didn't want to give Lisa permission to pass through. The officers had a discussion with the airport's head of security. They were adamant; Lisa was coming with them. Leaving the media behind at the security checkpoint, Serio's fellow officers—and Lisa—accompanied him and JJ to the gate and watched them board the plane. It was a show of solidarity not lost on Lisa and Serio, even amid their concern for JJ. Whatever squabbles there might have been among the K9 Squad handlers, there were no barriers when it came to doing everything they could for one another's dogs.

On the plane flight attendants hovered around while JJ either lay across the two seats next to Serio or curled up at his feet in the extra leg room of the bulkhead at the front of the plane. In midflight when JJ was fast asleep, Serio got up to use the restroom. JJ awoke to find Serio missing and walked through the aisle to find him, stopping to greet and slobber on passengers along the way.

Serio and JJ met Dr. Bergman at the Animal Medical Center in New York, and a team of veterinarians assessed and tested JJ for the program. Serio also met with the surgeon, who explained that they'd remove a large portion of the back of JJ's mouth and lymph nodes in his throat. They'd get as much of the tumor as possible, but due to the invasive nature of the cancer, complete resection might not be feasible. Radiation treatments would follow. JJ was scheduled for surgery two days later. They had time to kill in the Big Apple. Getting JJ to do his business occupied most of that time.

Staying on the eighteenth floor of the Sheraton New York Hotel, Serio and JJ rode the elevator and headed out to the concrete jungle. The sidewalks were crowded, but people from all walks of life, moving with purpose, often stopped in their tracks when they saw JJ. Unconcerned about dog hair and slobber, they showered him with pats and caresses, asking Serio what he was doing there. Some became emotional when they learned why.

JJ was particular about where he pooped and peed. Central Park, eight blocks away, was the only place he'd go. The interaction with people on the street was touching, and normally, the journey would be a pleasant stroll through some of New York's finest real estate, but arctic air had descended upon the city, and the average temperature for the week was twenty-eight degrees, the wind-chill factor making it feel closer to fifteen. JJ's feet froze up in the park, chunks of ice lodged between his pads.

Bergman and his medical team were kind to Serio and JJ, but it was a big veterinary hospital. Serio felt a little like a number. On the day of the surgery, they wanted Serio to drop JJ off.

"I don't do that," said Serio. "I'm normally with him whenever he's at the vet."

That wasn't an option. They would call him when the surgery ended.

There were no complications, but as the surgeon expected they couldn't remove all of the tumor. They wanted to keep JJ overnight. "We'll call you tomorrow, probably in the afternoon, and maybe you can come get him then."

"JJ has never stayed overnight in a hospital without me," said Serio. "He's not going to like being without his family there."

"He'll be fine," said the veterinary assistant. JJ would be so doped up on medication that he wouldn't know where he was.

• • •

Serio's hotel room phone rang at 8:00 a.m. "You can come get him," said one of the animal medical technicians.

"I thought you were going to keep him until the afternoon," said Serio, groggily.

"He's been howling and crying. It's like he's calling you."

JJ's constant baying was getting all the other dogs worked up.

Serio threw on a pair of jeans and ran the two miles to the veterinary hospital. They gave JJ's medication to Serio and said to watch him closely. JJ hadn't done his business the entire time he was there. As soon as they left the hospital, he pooped and peed all over the sidewalk.

They returned to the Animal Medical Center in New York three more times for JJ to receive radiation treatments and the experimental melanoma vaccine. JJ's veterinarian in Salt Lake City received special permission to administer a follow-up examination, saving them from having to make one final trip to New York. But they still needed to go for booster vaccinations every six months. The total price tag topped out at around fifteen thousand dollars.

In response to the numerous news reports and updates on JJ's progress, the Salt Lake City Police Department had received donations from all over Utah as well as from Nevada, California, Idaho, Montana, Virginia, and, somehow, New Zealand. An eleven-year-old girl named Megan Crowley, whose brother

Brandon had been found on the neighbor's porch by JJ the previous year, set up a lemonade stand to raise money for his cancer treatments. The generous outpouring covered nearly all of
JJ's expenses. A few Salt Lake police officers had spouses who
worked for JetBlue Airways. They contacted the airline's regional
director and told him about JJ. After the first trip to New York,
Serio received a call from JetBlue. "How many flights do you
need?" they asked, donating his remaining three flights to New
York, always putting him and JJ in the first row.

Unfortunately, JJ didn't always return the kindness.

The flight from Salt Lake City to New York takes a little over
four hours. It's a long time to sit in a steel tube hurtling thirty-
five thousand feet in the air, but people do it all the time. Now
imagine sitting captive in that tube for four hours while a bloodhound repeatedly farts. As a precaution Serio took JJ to the vet to
have his anal sacs squeezed before getting on the plane to New
York. It helped, but the medication that JJ was taking still gave
him horrendous gas. On one of the JetBlue flights, Serio heard
the flight attendants having a discussion near the forward galley.

"What's that smell?"

"Smells like something is burning."

Serio watched closely to make sure they weren't panicking
or going to notify the captain that something was wrong. He was
too embarrassed to tell them it was JJ, but he was prepared to if
necessary. Other passengers were also making comments about
the unknown smell, squinting their eyes.

• • •

On March 26, 2007, days after JJ's last trip to New York, the US
Department of Agriculture awarded conditional approval to the

canine melanoma vaccine. It was the first time the government ever had approved a therapeutic vaccine for the treatment of cancer either in animals or humans. The vaccine had helped numerous dogs in the study. JJ was one of them. The radiation treatments created a long gray streak on the right side of his face and neck, but his appetite returned, and his nose worked as well as ever. A week after surgery, before his next trip to New York, JJ was back on the police beat.

"That's what JJ lived for," said Lisa, about the decision for JJ to go back to work. "I felt like it was a good distraction for him. The trips to New York were stressful."

Serio also made it clear that JJ's happiness was the prime reason. Two weeks after his surgery, JJ caught yet another crime suspect hiding behind a dumpster. In an interview with the *Salt Lake Tribune* the next day, Serio said, "I'm doing this mainly for him. It's just a bonus that if he gets healthy he'll continue working."

On the night of April 5, Serio and JJ responded to a call to search for a stabbing suspect who had fled on foot. A man with a deep laceration on his right arm was bleeding profusely and being attended to by Officer Ben Johnson, who had called for an expedited medical response. An ambulance arrived quickly and rushed the man to the University Medical Center. A woman with a lacerated hand was also bleeding, but she refused medical help. Her boyfriend had beaten her and stabbed her friend when he tried to intervene.

With Serio and Johnson following, JJ picked up a track from the one-story brick house that led into the backyard and through the block. He scratched at a wooden gate and alerted on a yard. Serio opened the gate, and they found their suspect hiding deep within a crawl space less than two feet high beneath a wooden deck. They pulled him out and cuffed him. While they were taking him into custody, other officers at the scene entered the house where the stabbing occurred to conduct a protective sweep and see if anyone else was injured. They located fifty-four pounds of marijuana, 3.4 kilograms of cocaine, fourteen thousand dollars in cash, and several firearms.

A month later four individuals were up to no good, breaking into parked cars and stealing the contents. Around 2:00 a.m. Officer Jared Gilbert spotted the lookout man, who obviously wasn't doing his job. He dived behind a power pole to hide as one of his partners in crime yelled, "Cops!" They all scattered. Gilbert called for other units to respond. Officers located one of the suspects hiding on the ground next to a shed.

Serio deployed JJ at the house of a resident, who came outside when he heard something knocked over in his backyard and saw a man wearing all black running away. JJ tracked through an alley, over fences, and to the next block, bringing Serio to a suspect hiding underneath a table on the front porch of a house. The suspect's hands were bleeding from jumping fences. Serio, more prepared for the chase, wore gloves. Other officers took the suspect into custody. Serio brought JJ to another last sighting, and he picked up a track that passed three houses, went up a driveway, into a backyard, and behind a shed where another suspect was hiding. Serio and JJ repeated the steps and caught the third and final suspect.

Three suspects caught in three separate tracks on the same call—JJ's bout with cancer hadn't cost him a step. It did, however, take his voice away. When out on a track, every time JJ tried to bay, the sound was cut short or came out as a yelp, causing JJ some pain. Whether it was scar tissue or something to do with the radiation treatments, Serio didn't know. It also baffled the veterinarians, but it turned out to be a mystery that didn't need solving. By the time JJ received his first booster vaccination, his bay had returned.

STERN

The stern is long and tapering, and set on rather high, with a moderate amount of hair underneath.

October 2007

Born in the fall of 2007, Sammy J. completed the Serio family six-pack. Along with his big sister, Mikaela, he came home to a world inhabited by mellow four-legged monsters.

In the months before the melanoma, Serio and Lisa had been trying to have another baby. They could calculate a fertility window faster than a tollbooth worker could change a twenty-dollar bill. As any couple knows, the stress of trying to have a baby took the joy out of the journey. When they learned that JJ had cancer, they put aside their infertility problems, but they conceived Sammy the night before Serio left for JJ's first trip to New York.

In November JJ was diagnosed with cancer again, this time a tumor on his chest. The oral melanoma had gone into remission, so this was something new. To give JJ another chance, they elected for aggressive surgery to remove the growth and the surrounding area on his chest. The procedure removed most of JJ's signature white spot, but he bounced back quickly.

JJ was now ten years old, geriatric for a bloodhound. The average life expectancy of the breed ranges from ten to twelve years. But JJ was the Tony Bennett of bloodhounds. He might not have had the same speed or spring in his step, but he still had the spark, and he performed admirably. His tracking ability remained at the peak of his powers.

Employees working past midnight at convenience stores should receive hazard pay. Thieves and armed robbers targeted the 7-Elevens of the city, as well as the twenty-four-hour grocery stores. On January 8, 2008, Randy Brown, a clerk at Smith's Food and Drug, was taking a cigarette break around 2:30 a.m. The surgeon general warns on cigarette packages that "Quitting

JJ and Sammy
Photograph courtesy of Mike and Lisa Serio

Smoking Now Greatly Reduces Serious Risks to Your Health." The warning had lung cancer, heart disease, and emphysema in mind, but it also covered getting stabbed by an armed robber on your smoke break. Randy saw a white male wearing a black jacket enter the store. Two minutes later the man walked out of the store carrying two stolen frozen pizzas. Randy approached him, told him to go back inside, and grabbed the man's coat. The pizza thief swung around with a hunting knife and stabbed Randy in the side and back just below his armpit.

Jonathan Kelsey dropped the pizzas outside the grocery store and ran, but he held onto the knife. A witness saw him flee on foot to the east and disappear from view. Salt Lake County sheriff's officers arrived en masse. They requested assistance from other departments outside the jurisdiction, and officers, including several K9 teams, from South Salt Lake and the Murray Police Department came quickly. Last on the scene were three K9 officers from Salt Lake City with two German shepherds, Jinx and Apollo, and a bloodhound named JJ.

The Unified Fire Department treated Randy for his stab wound and took him to the Intermountain Medical Center in serious, but non-life-threatening condition. Salt Lake City K9 Officer Tony Brereton and Jinx detected an initial track near the store. County K9 Officer Kevin Barrett also deployed his shepherd, Vortex, in an area search. He found footprints in the snow between a trailer and a parked car that led to a fence. Next to the fence lay a black coat and a black-handled knife. Blood covered the curved blade. Barrett called for Serio and JJ.

JJ picked up a track from the knife and coat that led to a cinder-block wall separating a house from an auto parts store. Serio took JJ around the wall, where he reacquired the trail, which led into the neighborhood to the north. The sidewalk trail turned east through the neighborhood and hit South 700 East, a nine-lane highway. Without pause JJ crossed the highway, moving north with confidence. Cutting across asphalt, cement, packed gravel, and more major intersections, the trail continued for over two and a half miles, crossing into South Salt Lake City's jurisdiction and leading to a three-story apartment complex. JJ went up the steps to the second floor and paced back and forth, sniffing in front of three apartment doors. Serio radioed to report their location.

Meanwhile, investigators had determined that a gold Chevy pickup parked in front of the Smith's Food and Drug store was likely the suspect's vehicle. It was registered to Jonathan Kelsey and his father. Deputy Nathan Clark contacted Jonathan's father just after 3:00 a.m. His son had called him about twenty minutes previously, asking for a ride home, saying he had tried to steal beer from a store and ran away. Jonathan didn't mention anything about stabbing anyone. His father said he wouldn't help him. Investigators then traced the number Jonathan used to a cell phone belonging to Tyler Berenger.

South Salt Lake K9 Officer Matthew Jewkes recognized the name. Jewkes also knew that Berenger lived in the same apartment complex from which Serio had just radioed. Jewkes looked up Tyler's address and found he lived in apartment #11—one of the doors that JJ was sniffing.

Jewkes knocked on the door, and Berenger answered.

"Where's your cell phone?" Jewkes asked.

Berenger gestured to the living room table. The apartment was dark inside. Jewkes shone his flashlight into the living room and saw a man sleeping on the couch wearing a T-shirt spotted with blood. Jonathan Kelsey had a rude awakening: Jewkes and fellow officers ran inside and took him into custody.

John Henry, the steel-driving folk hero who raced a steam-powered hammer in a West Virginia rail tunnel and won, would have been proud. JJ's nose was old-school technology, tracing license plates and cell phone numbers the newer way to do it. The dog's track and the deputies' investigation complemented each other to achieve the same goal. That's what Serio had been striving to prove all along.

Certainly a convert, Officer Jon Richey was proselytizing his bloodhound beliefs as a part of the Salt Lake County Sheriff's Office. He had retired from the Salt Lake City Police Department four months prior and transferred to the county. In his last assignment for the city, he had worked as the detective sergeant over the Robbery Squad. Away from the K9 division for too long, Richey wanted to get back into it. He had handled German shepherds for seventeen years, so now he wanted to try a different breed. Serio and JJ had shown him what was possible. He just needed to convince his new department to add a bloodhound.

Richey pulled out his spreadsheets of patrol dog and bloodhound statistics to support his aims, but so far he hadn't had much luck. But seeing is believing. The Salt Lake County field commander, K9 sergeant, and all those who had influence in the sheriff's office happened to be at the scene the night that JJ tracked two and a half miles through difficult urban terrain right to the apartment complex where their stabbing suspect was hiding.

"You can hear a story like that, and it's neat," Richey said, "but it doesn't have near the impact that it does when you watch it. When you watch it happen, it's absolutely incredible."

Soon after, the Salt Lake County Sheriff's Office asked Richey to start a bloodhound program for their department.

• • •

The Watch Command Logs, noting the significant criminal cases each day in Salt Lake City, look much the same the year after JJ's melanoma diagnosis and surgery as they do in the years before. They teem with kudos to Serio and JJ:

- Aggravated Assault: Officer Serio and JJ were able to quickly find a track and found suspect hiding behind the dumpster at the Burger King on North Temple. Great job, JJ and Mike!!!

- Burglary: Officer Serio and sidekick JJ picked up a track shortly after arrival, which they worked over hill and dale. Officer Lennberg and K9 Troll hit on the two in their hiding spot.

- Felony Warrant: Officers Serio/JJ responded and picked up a track, worked it for 20 minutes for several hundred yards. Track went over several fences and led right up to the arrested person. Kudos once again to Officer(s) Serio and JJ for trailing and finding our suspect.

- DUI Hit and Run: Officer Serio deployed JJ and tracked suspect to house. Assisting officers circled the home and found suspect inside. As per usual, outstanding work by Mike and JJ.

On February 17 Bountiful Police Department officers were pursuing a stolen vehicle heading toward Salt Lake City. They requested assistance, then lost their visual on the car. Officer Nickolas Pierce spotted the abandoned vehicle, and Serio and JJ responded to do their job. JJ picked up the suspect's scent from the vehicle and tracked five blocks along the Jordan River parkway. He lost the trail for a little while but picked it up again. He pulled Serio up a driveway, sat down in front of a trash can, and bayed.

Serio kicked the trash can, which felt heavy. He opened the lid, revealing Rick Nieser curled up inside. It was the fifth or sixth time JJ had found someone hiding inside a garbage can. Two of those instances, oddly enough, were the same individual, a car prowler and habitual auto thief named Hoc Do. The first time JJ found Do in a trash can on the northwest side of the city, it took Serio a while to figure out that the scent trail ended right in front of him. A year later on the southeast side of the city, Serio was a little quicker on the uptake, but he was more surprised to find a familiar face among the trash.

"You've got to be kidding me," Serio said to Do. "Didn't you learn the first time that that doesn't work?"

"I would have gotten away except for that *damn* dog!" Do replied like some crook at the end of *Scooby-Doo*. It was familiar music to Serio's ears.

● ● ●

Serio had taken JJ to the UC–Davis School of Veterinary Medicine in California for his first six-month booster and again for his second in early March 2008. Before the trip JJ wasn't exhibiting any symptoms and enjoyed hiking in Tahoe along the way. Shortly after returning home, however, JJ's symptoms returned. He panted a lot and was having trouble breathing. Serio took him to the vet.

After taking a day or two to compose himself, Serio wrote an e-mail to the entire Salt Lake City Police Department.

To: Police (ALL)
Subject: JJ update

*I write to you about JJ, my K9 partner and best friend,
with an extremely heavy heart. JJ's cancer has returned and
is throughout his body. The vaccine treatments worked for
a year but for some reason have stopped. While fighting this
cancer, JJ tracked down almost 50 more criminals. His will
to work was simply amazing. Most importantly, my family
at home, my family at work, and I got to spend another year
with him. I thank you all for the support this past year and
over JJ's remarkable 8-plus-year career.*

*JJ will be at work with me when I am here. Being here
puts him at ease. I suspect he does not have very long, so
please come and make his tail wag a few more times.*

Sincerely,
Mike and JJ

• • •

Finding Rick Nieser in the trash can was JJ's final apprehension.
Sitting at Serio's side, he spent his last few days as a police dog
getting treats from his partners in blue.

Meanwhile, Lisa had been planning to visit family in Virginia
with Mikaela and Sammy. Serio's mom, JoAnne, had flown to
Utah to accompany Lisa back to Virginia and help with the logistics of traveling with a four-year-old and a five-month-old. An
Italian mother with all those stereotypical skills in the kitchen,
JoAnne Serio was famous for her meatballs. JJ and Josie were her
most ardent culinary fans.

"The two of them would not leave me alone in the kitchen," said JoAnne. "I'd yell at them, send them out of the kitchen area, and make them stay on the other side of the line. They'd sit there and stare at me and stare at me. When I finished, I'd always give them a reward of meatballs."

While JoAnne was visiting, JJ's condition took a turn for the worse. A week shy of his eleventh birthday, JJ kept walking around the house, trying to find a place where he could breathe more easily. Serio had rented an oxygenator from a nursing home, which helped a little, but JJ's body was overheating. With the windows wide open to let in the cold March air, Serio stayed up all night with JJ in the guest room downstairs. Early in the morning Serio took him outside for a short walk. For the first time in JJ's life, he didn't put his nose down to sniff the world. He stumbled, almost falling to the ground. Serio carefully sat him down on the sidewalk, and they looked out over the Salt Lake Valley, lighting up below them in the predawn hour.

There was nothing more he could do for his dog. Crying, Serio gave JJ a hug and a kiss, walked back in the house, and called for the vets.

Dr. Kris Muscari, JJ's primary veterinarian, and her husband, Dr. Tim Hassinger, who had provided medical care for JJ even before the police department covered his routine procedures, were good friends with Serio and Lisa. Both doctors had come over for dinner with their two kids only a week earlier. When Serio called, Muscari and Hassinger said they'd be at the house as soon as possible. While waiting for them to arrive, Serio wrapped JJ in a blanket and took him to their bed, JJ's favorite comfort spot. He offered JJ some of his mom's meatballs with sauce. As sick as JJ was, he ate two of them from Serio's hand.

"Am I doing the right thing?" Serio asked over and over, to Lisa, his mom, Muscari, and Hassinger. They all agreed that he was. As the veterinarians prepared to euthanize JJ, Lisa held on to Serio at the side of the bed while JoAnne stayed downstairs with the kids.

JJ had a panicked look in his eyes, making Serio wish he could explain what was happening and why. When Muscari inserted the IV line in JJ's front leg, the dog cried out and jerked away. The last thing Serio wanted was for JJ to feel any more pain. When the vets got the line in a back leg, JJ calmed down a little, but he still looked scared. Serio wanted to hold him, but he knew that wouldn't help. Instead, he did something better.

As Muscari administered the injection, Serio asked his partner a question with as much positive inflection as he could manage: "JJ, do you want to go to *work?*"

JJ tilted his head the way he always did when asked. With a look of anticipation in his eyes, ready for one final track, JJ's heart stopped beating.

From downstairs JoAnne heard her son scream. "It was horrible," she said. "When they gave the shot to JJ, it was like they took Mike's soul. It was the saddest thing I've ever lived through because I knew how much it pained him to do that."

• • •

Over the next few days, friends and coworkers came by the house to offer their condolences. Serio had taken JJ's body to a crematorium. He kept some of the ashes in a special box, spreading the rest over some of JJ's favorite spots in the Salt Lake Valley.

Alone one day, he took some of JJ's ashes up the mountain behind their house where they often went hiking. Taking Josie out sometime later that week, she went up the mountain and tracked right to the ashes. She missed JJ, too. When Josie had last had her teeth cleaned, she had to be drugged for the procedure. Still woozy from the medication when she came home, hardly able to stand, her head bobbed up and down. JJ approached her and very gently licked her eyes and face over and over. Serio had never seen him do that before. It was as if, from JJ's many experiences with medical procedures, he was telling her, "I know how it feels; you'll be all right."

The outpouring of sympathies from the police department, the news media, and the community overwhelmed Serio and his family. They knew JJ touched a lot of lives, but they couldn't anticipate the recognition he received. The Salt Lake City police team competing in the Baker to Vegas Relay—a 120-mile race from Baker, California, to Las Vegas, Nevada—wanted to run in honor of JJ and called themselves Team 1010, J being the tenth letter of the alphabet. For the Armed Forces Memorial Day Service at the Mountain View Cemetery, honoring the 125 Utah police officers who had died in the line of duty since 1853, officials added a special memorial service for JJ. Josie bayed in the middle of Serio's eulogy, and a full cadre of police officers followed the wail of bagpipes in a procession to JJ's memorial marker, a giant marble slab with a large copper plaque inscribed with pictures of JJ and an eloquent epitaph lauding his accomplishments.

Funny stories of JJ on the job and roaming the halls of the department helped lighten the pain of loss. Serio had often brought JJ into the dispatch room at the start or end of a graveyard shift, where the dispatch officers gave JJ lots of fattening contraband that he rarely if ever got from Serio. Now the officers shared some of their fondest memories:

Josie, Mikaela, Sammy, Serio, and Junior at JJ's memorial marker
Photograph courtesy of Mike and Lisa Serio

- "I'll always think of JJ every time I eat McDonald's french fries. I swear he could sniff out a bag of fries in a tornado!"

- "Just know that other agencies would call up and ask if JJ was on instead of just asking for a K9."

- "I'm sorry I won't have the privilege of being slobbered on, leaned against, or licked to death one more time. He will forever remain in my heart and mind as a friend and one hell of a never-give-up cop."

• • •

Serio received the Salt Lake City Officer of the Year Award in 2008, making him the only repeat winner in department history. But this time JJ got equal billing. The bloodhound received lots of credit when Serio won the award in 2001, but in 2008 the award specifically recognized "the dedicated service of JJ and his handler, Officer Mike Serio, and recognizes them as the Police Chief's Officers of the Year." With nearly fifty criminal captures in their final year together, Serio and JJ certainly deserved the annual award, but citing "the apprehension of 271 wanted persons during JJ's almost nine years of service" gave the honor the added burnish of a lifetime achievement award for JJ.

"What a thrill it was to show up on a scene not having a clue as to where the bad guy had gone until JJ put his nose to work," said Serio in his remarks. "Thank you, JJ, for letting me be a part of that. He deserves the award. I just ran with him for eight and half years."

GAIT

The gait is elastic, swinging and free, the stern being carried high, but not too much curled over the back.

May 2008

After JJ's death Serio took a few weeks off to adapt to life without JJ. It was hard to make it through the day, but he eventually returned and brought Josie along, more as a companion at first.

Randy Hunnewell and Moe were handling most of the calls involving a bloodhound, and a new K9 handler named Tyler Lowe had begun working with his young bloodhound, Chase. The year before, Serio and JJ had accompanied Lowe to Colorado, where they helped pick Chase from the litter, much as they had for Wyatt, Max, and Moe, the other three police bloodhounds working in the Salt Lake Valley. When JJ was first diagnosed with melanoma, Serio and the department started planning for his replacement. As a patrol officer Lowe had tried to get on calls whenever JJ was tracking. Some officers brought JJ good luck, and he always tracked right to the suspect. Lowe's presence had the opposite effect.

"All the times I was ever on a call with Mike, I don't think we ever caught a guy," said Lowe. "But it was a blast to follow his dog and hear him bay. I thought it was incredible."

Serio didn't begrudge Lowe for cooling his dog's luck. Most of the applicants for open K9 positions wanted to work with German shepherds, so Serio knew that Lowe was different and talked to him at length about bloodhounds. While Lowe was still working patrol, they picked up eleven-week-old Chase and began his education. For the first six months of training, Chase learned at the feet of the master. JJ taught by example.

Still assigned to the K9 Squad shortly after JJ's death, Serio worked Josie on a few calls to ride out his time until the next shift change, a month away. Emotionally, he was done. He couldn't envision working regularly with any other dog than JJ. He put

JJ's legacy: Salt Lake City Officer Tyler Lowe and Chase, South Jordan Officer Allen Crist and Wyatt, Salt Lake City Officer Randy Hunnewell and Moe, South Salt Lake Officer Alan Hunsaker and Max, Salt Lake City Officer Mike Serio and Josie, Unified Officer Jon Richey and Oliver, and West Valley Officer Shane Matheson and Copper.
Photograph courtesy of Salt Lake City Police Department

Recent Salt Lake City K9 Squad (from left to right): Officer Serio and Junior, Officer Lowe and Chase, Officer Peterson and Vader, Officer Brereton and Jinx, Sergeant Cameron and Apollo, Officer Lennberg and Thago (not shown: Officer Hunnewell and bloodhound Moe).
Photograph courtesy of Salt Lake City Police Department

in his bid for the afternoon shift as a patrol officer. Serio was returning to his rookie roots.

Lisa and Serio wanted to show their appreciation to everyone who had helped during the difficult times with JJ's cancer. Not all police dogs needing similar medical treatments received the same kind of support and attention. In the Salt Lake Valley, police departments don't provide financial assistance for veterinary care once a police service dog has retired. Along with the transfer of ownership from the department—and a symbolic one-dollar payment for the dog from the handler—comes the burden of medical care. Police departments also have limits on incurring costs for dogs on active duty. Sometimes dogs are euthanized because of the financial constraints of the police department or handler.

Recognizing a need, Lisa and Serio established JJ's Police Dog Fund. They kicked in a few thousand dollars of their own money to get it started and began raising funds for the cause, relying on the continued generosity of others who wanted to give the police dogs a chance to receive the care and dignity that they had earned in their years of protecting and serving the community.

Elvis, JJ's old working buddy, became the first beneficiary of the fund. Retired from service in Officer Lennberg's care, Elvis had stomach bloat, a potentially life-threatening condition that, in his case, required emergency surgery. An outlay from JJ's Police Dog Fund helped ease the cost. A short time later another retired German shepherd needed surgery, this time to remove a tumor. For nine years Erik had worked with Officer Glenn Smith for South Salt Lake. JJ's fund once again helped a shepherd enjoy his rightful retirement of sleeping all day and running after balls instead of criminals.

After two weeks back on patrol, Serio had elective knee surgery, which he had been putting off for far too long. Years of jumping fences coupled with year-round soccer games had taken their toll. In the care of the same surgeon who had recently worked on Tiger Woods's knee, Serio was confident he'd be back stronger than ever. The surgery revealed more damage than anticipated, though, and instead of three weeks, Serio was on short-term disability for nearly three months.

While Serio convalesced, others conspired. "This is crazy," said Randy Hunnewell, talking to K9 sergeant Eddie Cameron. "We're losing a wealth of training and experience by letting Serio go." After switching to patrol Serio had continued to help out with training, working with Hunnewell, Lowe, and their bloodhounds, Moe and Chase. But Hunnewell knew that wasn't the same as being there on a regular basis.

"At best he's a marginal cop," said Hunnewell bluntly, referring to Serio as a patrol officer. "He'll never be a great cop, but he'll always be a great K9 guy. As a resource he's irreplaceable."

Funding a K9 position is an expensive undertaking. The biggest obstacles are start-up costs: buying the truck, outfitting the truck, buying the dog, training dog and handler. Hunnewell made the case to anybody who listened. "Right now we've got the truck and the equipment," he said, "and in Serio we've got a handler already trained, and he's got a dog in Josie that's already trained and operational. The only thing the department has to provide is the extra contractual stipend for K9."

Other obstacles included tradition and whether Serio wanted to come back to K9. Standard procedure in the police department had officers move on to other assignments after a set period of time. For K9 officers that usually happened after their dog retired, giving others a chance so departments stay fresh and allow officers to move through the organization.

"I never want to say to anybody," said Chief Burbank, "you're so valuable in this assignment that I don't want you to do something else. You always want to give your employees a chance to move up." In the days after Serio decided to move to patrol, a number of officers approached Burbank and told him, "You need to keep Mike Serio in the bloodhound program to make it successful." Burbank took particular note of the sentiment from the other K9 handlers. Specialty assignments such as K9 have a limited headcount, in essence making Serio the competition. "To have them come and say we want him to stay is, in our profession, one of the highest compliments that can be paid," said Burbank.

It wasn't an easy choice for Serio, but for everyone who knew him it was a foregone conclusion. At the end of the summer, when his knee had healed enough to report back to duty, he returned not to patrol but to the K9 Squad.

"I think Mike would do it without pay," said Chief Burbank. "You can't pay those kinds of people enough. I've got a motor officer who has been around for twenty-plus years. He's the highest producer and loves to be out there. He writes more tickets than anyone. He'd write his own mother, but yet I have people come and tell me all the time, 'He was so nice when he wrote me that speeding ticket.' That's the way Mike is for the K9 program. His passion is there, and when you can find that, it makes my job that much easier because I don't worry about the program."

With Josie at his side, Serio continued with the K9 Squad. The only people who disliked the new arrangement were the criminals that Josie was catching—and Lisa. Her consulting job allowed Lisa to work from home, and she was used to having Josie always at her side.

Serio had trained Josie from the time she was a puppy and brought her on many working nights. She had good tracking skills, but in her heart of hearts she was a homebody. She had been out of the loop for too long. She did find some suspects, but she didn't have the same drive that JJ had. Although Josie wasn't a stellar tracker, Serio never once felt guilty about working with her. JJ had known and loved her. Only six months had passed since JJ's death—too early to consider a replacement partner.

Serio's dad, always an anchor in his life, had a different take on the matter. "You lost your partner," Joe Serio told his son, "but you still have your skill set that JJ passed on to you as a handler. To do justice, not only for yourself but for JJ, you have to go get another bloodhound."

Every revolutionary needs a goal. Serio had achieved his goal of enrolling a bloodhound in the Salt Lake City Police Department. "I used to dream about just catching one bad guy," said Serio, "I had no idea we'd catch so many." More than that, JJ's impact had made waves. Five other police bloodhounds were working in the valley, with more on the way. *Why doesn't every police department in the country have a bloodhound?* he thought. Serio had a new goal.

"They wouldn't know how to operate without a bloodhound being on call," Chief Burbank said of his men. "It's just become a part of what we have, just like the gun on your hip or the handcuff in your case." That's how Serio saw the role of a bloodhound: a useful tool that should be in every police toolbox. As with a gun, an officer didn't need a bloodhound in every case, but it was useful to have one when the need arose. Serio wanted to send the message that the need arose more often than most police departments ever realized.

Bloodhounds are rare in police K9 squads throughout the country, and even in the majority of departments where they do work, they are deployed sparingly. Often, a K9 handler has a bloodhound at home and deploys that dog only when requested. But Serio and the other bloodhound handlers in the Salt Lake area worked their dogs differently. They had their hounds with them at all times, worked at night when more crimes happened and scent contamination was lowest, and got to the scene in most cases within twenty minutes, when the scent trail was fresh.

Serio had also seen the limitations. A dog could follow scent trails many hours old in a rural setting with lots of undisturbed vegetation, but in urban environments, where chemicals and oils contaminate the ground and the air swirls with currents of other people's scents and gases from cars, trucks, buses, and trains, that became extremely unlikely. Nevertheless, time and again bloodhound handlers—some of them recognized experts in the field—claimed that their dogs could consistently follow trails more than twelve hours old in the city. "In all the seminars I've been to, they can't," said Serio. "Some will actually say, 'I can't run this trail, it's too fresh.'"

He could win the battle only if people saw past the myth to the reality, focusing not on outlandish claims but on how good bloodhounds can be when trained properly and deployed in the right conditions. He was still working Josie and having some success, but Serio realized—after everyone else who knew him already had—that to fight in the battle he needed another bloodhound partner.

Richey, the renowned German shepherd handler who switched to bloodhounds, needed a new and lighter dog because Oliver, his current bloodhound, weighed over a hundred pounds. Richey's bad back prevented him from pushing the hefty boy over fences without pain. Richey and Serio drove to the farm of breeders Dave and Brenda Daniher in La Junta, Colorado.

Cisco, the sire of the puppies, worked with a handler for the Colorado State Prison system. The dam—reportedly a fine tracking dog—belonged to a civilian handler. Richey picked out a spry and confident female puppy and named her Molly. Serio went through his rigorous procedures of testing each dog for curiosity, independence, and drive. The Danihers probably wouldn't have been surprised if Serio pulled out Rorschach inkblots to test the puppies, but he finally made a choice: a wandering, wrinkly, black-and-tan, eight-week-old male with a jaunty gait.

When Richey went to pay for Molly, the Danihers charged him about seven hundred dollars. For Serio, however, Dave and Brenda told him, "You don't have to pay anything. We're going to donate the dog to you." They had read about JJ. "We're just honored that you'll be working one of our dogs in the city."

Richey had no reason to hold a grudge. Shortly after JJ died, an attorney taken with JJ's story called Serio. The man wanted to donate ten thousand dollars to support the bloodhound program and get more police dogs working in the Salt Lake Valley. Serio wasn't ready then and didn't plan on returning to K9. He told the attorney about Richey, who had started a bloodhound program for the Salt Lake County Sheriff's Office. A ten-thousand-dollar check helped establish Friends for Salt Lake County K9, a nonprofit organization that has helped Richey and a lot of other handlers and their dogs. JJ's legacy is still paying dividends long after his death.

Partly to track bloodlines, but also as a point of prestige, the American Kennel Club certifies the names of purebred dogs in the United States. Serio and Lisa never had any doubt about what to name their new puppy. His AKC-certified name is JJ's Legacy Junior.

He goes by Junior, for short.

EPILOGUE

LEGACY

August 2011

"Charlie 254, I was almost just hit by a vehicle at 800 East 2100 South," called Officer Jacob Nattress over the radio. A silver Subaru Impreza blowing through a red light at high speed nearly T-boned Nattress's patrol car at an intersection around 1:30 a.m. He flipped on his emergency lights. "I'm turning around to try to catch it. Vehicle is traveling northbound, obviously fleeing. I'm not pursuing."

Like many other police departments, Salt Lake City has a restrictive pursuit policy. Officers didn't pursue a fleeing vehicle unless they knew it was an aggravated felony situation. The logic of the policy encased a balancing act, with public safety at the fulcrum. High-speed pursuits involve high risks, which the police are willing to take only if violent crimes against people have taken place. Endangering lives pursuing a stolen car isn't worth it. Nattress didn't know if the driver was under the influence or just driving erratically. He lost sight of the car.

Serio and Sergeant Dave Wierman were both working that night, and each drove to the area to help in the search. About ten minutes later Wierman found the car, and Serio came right away.

"I believe I've located the vehicle that fled from 254," said Wierman, calling dispatch. "It's on 710 East Wilson Avenue. Kilo 854 starting a track from here. Have crime lab ready to process. I'm gonna stay with the car. We need one more officer to stay with 854."

Serio scented his dog off the driver's seat of the abandoned Subaru, and Junior picked up a track heading east, passing two houses before turning south through a dark alley splitting the block into two halves. Serio didn't have backup yet, but he wasn't too concerned. Another officer was on the way, and he was tracking suspects who probably had just stolen a car. Junior tracked across the next street into a lot behind some commercial property.

"Metro 694, Taylorsville had a shooting involving suspects that match the description of the males that fled, approximately thirty minutes ago. Both 10-88."

Now Serio was concerned. "10-88" means armed and dangerous. Metro Gang officers had been looking for suspects who had stolen a rifle out of a Unified Police Department officer's vehicle. The radio announcement linked the suspects to the home invasion armed robbery that had just occurred in Taylorsville and the abandoned vehicle where Junior had started his track.

"Kilo 854, have them expedite," Serio said, calling for company. "I'm just south of the Classic Cleaners on Lake Street. I'm real hot." Right on cue, Junior bayed. He wanted to find what he was looking for and didn't like being held back.

Wierman got in his car and left the abandoned vehicle. With armed and dangerous suspects on the loose, helping Serio trumped watching the car. He drove ahead of Serio's position. "210, I'll be holding on Ramona Avenue and Lake Street, but the next officer needs to meet up with 854."

Two Metro Gang officers met up with Serio and Junior.

"Kilo 854, he went over the fence just south of the Classic Cleaners. We're going to get over the fence and see if the track continues. Get some units directly over there on Lake Street. See if we can pin him down."

Ivy covered the tall chain-link fence, too high for Serio to boost Junior over, but it was loose at the bottom. The two Metro Gang officers lifted it up, and Junior scooted underneath the fence. Serio crawled under after him and was pulled up to his feet as Junior hit the track and lunged forward. Serio let him continue, figuring the Metro Gang officers would climb the fence and catch up soon. He had no idea it would happen so quickly.

In the pitch-dark lot, Serio shone his flashlight ahead. About forty yards away, he caught a glimpse of a figure that popped up out of the brush and ran.

"Police!" Serio yelled.

The suspect ran southeast across Lake Street. Serio dropped Junior's leash and ran after him. Junior, nose to the ground when Serio ran past him, caught up and grabbed his partner's left hand in his mouth, holding him back. The hound hadn't spotted the suspect yet, probably thinking that Serio was playing a game with him.

The dispatch officer sounded the triple beep. "All units, be advised: Foot pursuit southbound on Lake Street approaching Ramona Avenue."

Serio kept yelling "Police!" as he ran and even threw in, "I'm going to send my dog," as Junior was running freely alongside him. The suspect continued running, but Serio was closing fast. He drew his weapon and yelled for the man to drop to the ground. The suspect, assumed to be armed and dangerous, didn't comply. Serio made a quick decision he wasn't going to shoot the guy, but he had to keep hold of his gun. When he got within reach, he pushed the suspect with his left hand and swung overtop with his right. His fist and gun struck the man in the head, knocking him to the ground. The two Metro Gang officers caught up and joined the tackle. They cuffed the guy while Junior jumped around and bayed at the moon. Officers captured the suspect's armed accomplice the next day.

● ● ●

Serio and Junior
Photograph courtesy of Salt Lake City Police Department

Junior is Salt Lake City's fourth bloodhound. When JJ began, he was the lone police bloodhound in Utah for five years before some floppy-eared company joined him. Over the last years of JJ's life, four other bloodhounds added their noses to the Salt Lake region's police departments. Since then eleven more blood-hounds have joined the Salt Lake Valley's K9 ranks. From zero to sixteen; JJ's legacy not only endures—it's growing.

Half of the catalyst is still a part of it.

"Some people have convinced us of a new way of thinking," said Terry Fritz, Special Operations deputy chief. "We've come back to the Fortune 500 company business philosophy: If you have a productive, above-and-beyond-their-numbers salesper-son, you don't mandatorily rotate them just because that's the standard. As long as Mike is producing and happy and having fun, we're going to keep him. He'll probably spend his entire career there. With a young dog, he could easily do that. And why not?"

Junior's first find as a police dog was an intoxicated seventeen-year-old male. Along with friends the boy brought his girlfriend back to her house at 3:00 a.m. The girl's father, upset and no doubt not seeing son-in-law material, told the youth that his daughter wouldn't be going out with him again. The kid didn't take the news well. He and a friend threw a beer can and a log at the girl's father before fleeing. Junior tracked him through multi-ple neighborhood blocks to a residence a half mile away. Such a relatively small crime normally wouldn't make it into the Watch Command Log, but Lieutenant Fred Louis noted the significance: "Simple Assault: Great job by Serio and Junior; this was Junior's first capture and second deployment. This was fantastic work by such a young (only five months old) police service dog. It looks like another great partnership/career is about to begin."

Over JJ's storied career—in addition to all the joy and energy he brought to those who knew him—he averaged 32 criminal apprehensions a year. In his namesake's first three and a half years on the streets of Salt Lake City, Junior has taken credit for 110 apprehensions, an average of 31 per year. He's one step behind and closing. With never a competitive bone in his body, JJ would love the company.

ACKNOWLEDGMENTS

In writing, knowing where to begin is always the hardest, but in this case it's pretty easy. Officer Michael Serio—full disclosure at the end—has been a great friend since we were twelve-year-old military brats living in Stuttgart, Germany. As long as you don't mind somebody stealing all of your Lucky Charms cereal, he's also one of the best college roommates a guy could have. I am grateful to Mike and Lisa for their lasting friendship and hosting me on my many trips to Salt Lake City. I might have helped kick off their dog craze with Jessie, but they've taken it to a whole new level with JJ, Josie, and Junior.

My gratitude, also, to the Salt Lake City Police Department for introducing me to, and having me sign beneath, the longest sentence I have ever had the pleasure of reading.

Now, therefore, in consideration of the permission given to me to ride in a vehicle assigned to the Salt Lake City Police Department and to accompany a member of said Department during the performance of his/her/their official duties, I do hereby agree that I am aware that the work of the Police Department is inherently dangerous and that I may be subjected to the risk of death, personal injury, or damage to my property by accompanying a member(s) of the Police Department during the performance of his/her/their official duties I freely, voluntarily, and with such knowledge, assume the risk of death, personal injury, or property damage arising from or in any way connected with accompanying a member of the Police Department

*including, but not restricted to, the use of weapons, lawful
or unlawful acts or forcible resistance by law violators
or suspected law violators, assault, riot, breach of the
peace, fire, explosion, gas, electrocution or the escape of
radioactive substances, or automobile accidents while
accompanying a member(s) of the Salt Lake City Police
Department during the performance of his/her/their official
duties.*

I have the utmost respect for the incredible job that police
officers do on a daily basis and thank the many law enforce-
ment personnel in the Salt Lake Valley who shared their sto-
ries. Their professionalism and candor helped provide colorful
details and piece together the narrative. In particular, I thank
Chief Chris Burbank, Chief Scott Folsom, Retired Chief Mike
Roberts, Deputy Chief Terry Fritz, Retired Captain Judy Dencker,
Lieutenant Dave Cracroft, Lieutenant Craig Gleason, Lieutenant
Melody Gray, Lieutenant Glenn Smith, Sergeant David Wierman,
Sergeant Kelly Kent, Sergeant Brad Marshal, Sergeant Allen Crist,
K9 Officer Jon Richey, K9 Officer Randy Hunnewell, and K9 Offi-
cer Tyler Lowe. I am also grateful to Jeff Schettler for allowing
me to observe and lay trail for his Police K9 Mantrailing Seminar
in Placerville, California.

Thanks also to Joe Serio, JoAnne Serio, and Adam Childs for
sharing stories both heartfelt and heartbreaking.

I am blessed with being a part of a wonderful writing community. I thank all those who provided sugar with the medicine,
sharing constructive criticism while making it seem like compliments. For their extraordinary grace and kindness, I especially
thank Scott Evans, Raychel Kubby Adler, David Lloyd Sutton, Rich
and Kathy Williams, Kate Montieth, Susan Walker, Lisa Slabach,

Ron Lane, Peggy Froehlich, Don Schwartz, Valerie Fioravanti, Rae Gouirand, participants in the Brenda Miller Workshop, and members of the Blue Moon Writers Guild.

I offer special thanks to my agent, Jill Marsal of the Marsal Lyon Literary Agency, for helping me see the light early on. She's right: It's not a true crime story; it's a book about a dog. I am indebted also to my editor, James Jayo at Lyons Press, for aiding and abetting me in the murder, as Quiller-Couch put it, of my darlings. His encyclopedic knowledge and attention to craft and accuracy significantly improved the telling.

Thanks to my mom and dad, Mary Jean and Sam Russ, for the love and solid foundation and my three older brothers: John for softening the rules, Sam for letting me borrow his Conan books, and Eric for beating me just enough that I had nothing to fear by comparison from the class bully. Lastly and most especially, I offer thanks to Kadee, my partner in life and love, and our son, Atticus, who brings me joy every day no matter the weather.

NOTES AND SOURCES

Following are the main sources for each chapter; they don't list the source of every quotation, anecdote, and fact. This book was informed in large part by interviews and correspondence with principal characters, direct observations of police K9 teams at work in Utah and California, and research drawn from police files, books, newspapers, magazines, websites, manuals, handouts, letters, memos, and e-mail correspondence.

Introduction

Primary sources in this section include interviews and correspondence with Chief Chris Burbank, Deputy Chief Terry Fritz, Sergeant Kelly Kent, and K9 Officer Michael Serio.

Note: Some experts who work with scent dogs distinguish between "tracking" and "trailing." Tracking, they believe, is when a dog follows odors caused by ground disturbance—that is, scents arising from crushed vegetation or displaced soil. Trailing, on the other hand, is when a dog follows an individual's unique scent—pheromones and shed cells. The public commonly uses the term "tracking" when referring to scent dogs such as bloodhounds. The many K9 handlers I interviewed and observed at work in both Utah and California used "tracking" and "trailing" interchangeably for the most part. Deferring to their expertise, I treat the terms similarly.

Andrew Beahrs, *Twain's Feast: Searching for America's Lost Foods in the Footsteps of Samuel Clemens* (New York, New York: The Penguin Press, 2010).

"Blake Shelton: Celebrating Country Life," *Ada Evening News* (April 25, 2009).

James "Bo" Bohan, Don Goodman, and Mark Sherrill, "Ol' Red." First sung by George Jones on album *You Oughta Be Here with Me* (Epic, 1990).

Simon de Bruxelles, "Bloodhounds to Pick Up the Trail After 60 Years," *Times* (London) (December 29, 1998).

Otto Erich Deutsch, *Mozart: A Documentary Biography* (Stanford University Press, 1965).

Rawdon B. Lee, *A History and Description of the Modern Dogs of Great Britain and Ireland, Sporting Division, Vol. 1* (1894). Excerpt from *The Bloodhound: A Complete Anthology of the Dog* (Vintage Dog Books, 2010).

William Poundstone, *Prisoner's Dilemma* (New York, New York: Doubleday, 1992).

Chapter 1

Primary sources in this chapter include interviews and correspondence with K9 Officer Jon Richey, K9 Officer Randy Hunnewell, and K9 Officer Michael Serio.

Marc Haddock, "Salt Lake Streets Have Seen Many Changes Over Past 150 Years," *Deseret News* (July 13, 2009).

Salt Lake City Police Department, Case Number 2003-201212, General Occurrence Hardcopy; Initial Responding Officer Report by Merrill Alan Stuck, Field Supplemental Reports by Cale B. Lennberg and Michael Serio.

US Census Bureau, *2010 Census of Population,* Population Estimates Program (July 1, 2011).

Chapter 2

Primary sources in this chapter include interviews and correspondence with Lisa Serio and K9 Officer Michael Serio.

Note: Scientists often take pride in calling their particular field of expertise an "exact science," in which quantitative accuracy rules the day and hypotheses can be rigorously tested. That said, they don't always agree, and at least for those who study the science of scent, the space between where they stake their conclusions can form a vast chasm. Olfactory receptors in the cell membranes of the nose allow for the detection of odor molecules in the air—the more olfactory receptors, the greater the sense of smell. Depending on which study you believe, humans have anywhere from five to forty million olfactory receptors in our sniffers. Based on those same discordant studies, your average dog possesses anywhere from one hundred million to one billion, and the bloodhound nose logs in with a range between three hundred million and four billion olfactory receptors. Wide disparities aside, all the studies agree that a dog's nose is significantly more powerful than a human's, and the bloodhound is top dog of them all. It's no wonder that the bloodhound is sometimes called a nose with a dog attached.

American Kennel Club, *2010 Dog Registration Statistics Historical Comparisons & Notable Trends,* www.akc.org/reg/dogreg_stats .cfm.

Lillian R. Aronson, Daniel J. Brockman, and Dorothy Cimino Brown, "Gastrointestinal Emergencies," *The Veterinary Clinics of North America,* Volume 30 (2000).

John Barbour, *The Bruce* (1375).

Karen Becker, "When to Induce Vomiting in Pets," *Healthy Pets with Dr. Karen Becker* (May 15, 2011).

Corey Binns, "How We Smell," *Live Science* (May 22, 2006).

T. Birch, *Boyle's Life and Works,* vol. 3 (1772).

Blind Harry, *The Actes and Deidis of the Illustre and Vallyeant Campioun Schir William Wallace* (1470).

Bookrags.com, *Introduction to Uncle Tom's Cabin Study Guide.*

Robert Boyle, *Of the Determinate Nature of Effluviums* (1673).

Catherine F. Brey and Lena F. Reed, *The New Complete Bloodhound* (New York: Howell Book House, 1991).

Charles IX, *La Chasse Royale,* chaps. 7 and 8 (1625).

Stanley Coren, "The Human-Canine Bond," *Psychology Today* (January 15, 2011).

A. Cunningham, P. Manis, P. Reed, and G. Ronnett, "Olfactory receptor neurons exist as distinct subclasses of immature and mature cells in primary culture," *Neuroscience* 93:4 (1999).

Gallagher Flinn, "10 Best Family Dog Breeds," The Learning Channel.

Mietje Germonpré, et al., "Fossil Dogs and Wolves from Palaeolithic Sites in Belgium, the Ukraine and Russia: Osteometry, Ancient DNA and Stable Isotopes," *Journal of Archaeological Science* 36:2 (February 2009).

Ellen J. Goldner, "Arguing with Pictures: Race, Class and the Formation of Popular Abolitionism Through Uncle Tom's Cabin," *Journal of American & Comparative Cultures* 24 (2001).

Ira N. Levine, *Physical Chemistry* (New York: McGraw-Hill, 1978).

Laurie Maguire, Dog Breed Info Center, www.dogbreedinfo.com/articles/caninebloat.htm.

"Underdogs: The Bloodhound's Amazing Sense of Smell," *Nature* (PBS, June 23, 2008).

John Paul Scott and John L. Fuller, *Dog Behavior: The Genetic Basis* (Chicago: University of Chicago Press, 1974).

D. Shier, J. Butler, and R. Lewis, *Hole's Human Anatomy & Physiology* (Boston: McGraw-Hill, 2004).

Martha Stewart, "Top 10 Dog Breeds," www.marthastewart.com/275479/top-10-dog-breeds/@center/307037/dog-breeds-center#/220822.

Harriet Beecher Stowe, *Uncle Tom's Cabin* (Dover Thrift Editions, 2005).

Regina M. Sullivan, "Review: Olfaction in the Human Infant" (Sense of Smell Institute, July 2000).

William G. Syrotuck, *Scent and the Scenting Dog* (Mechanicsburg, Pennsylvania: Barkley Productions, 2000).

Kim Campell Thornton, *Bloodhounds: A Complete Pet Owner's Manual* (Barron's Educational Series, 1998).

"The Top 20 Best Dog Breeds for Children," www.squidoo.com/top-20-best-dog-breeds-for-children.

University of Virginia, "Uncle Tom's Cabin on Film," *Uncle Tom's Cabin and American Culture,* a Multi-Media Archive.

Geoffrey Wheatcroft, "The Cousins' War: review of Amanda Foreman, 'A World on Fire,'" *New York Times Book Review* (July 3, 2011).

Chapter 3

Primary sources in this chapter include interviews and correspondence with Lisa Serio, Joe Serio, JoAnne Serio, K9 Officer Jon Richey, and K9 Officer Michael Serio.

American Kennel Club, *AKC Meet the Breeds: Bloodhound* (February 29, 1996).

National Police Bloodhound Association, www.npba.com.

Kim Campbell Thornton, *Bloodhounds: A Complete Pet Owner's Manual* (Barron's Educational Series, 1998).

Bill Tolhurst, *Police Pocket Training Manual for Bloodhound Handlers,* 1st ed. (National Police Bloodhound Association, 1990).
United Schutzhund Clubs of America, *Traits of Schutzhund Dogs.*

Chapter 4

Primary sources in this chapter include interviews and correspondence with Adam Childs, Chief Chris Burbank, and K9 Officer Michael Serio.

Bruce Ludemann, Jr., *Home of the Big T: The Man Behind It All,* www
.angelfire.com/ny4/bigT.
Nebraska State Historical Society, *William Jennings Bryan, 1860–1925* (February 25, 2011), www.nebraskahistory.org/lib-arch/
research/manuscripts/politics/bryanwj.htm.
Jack Shuler, *Our Qualifications,* Jackshuler.com.
———, *Shuler Bloodhounds: Mantrailing I Training Seminar,*
Handout (November 5, 1998).
ThinkExist.com Quotations, "Oliver Wendell Holmes quotes,"
(ThinkExist.com Quotations: July 1, 2012), http://en.thinkexist
.com/quotes/oliver_wendell_holmes.
Bill Tolhurst, *The Police Textbook for Dog Handlers* (Bill Tolhurst, 1991).
———, *Scent Transfer Unit: STU-100* (Tolhurst Big "T" Enterprises,
1991), www.angelfire.com/ny4/bigT/STU100.html.
———, *The Silent Witness: Scent.* (Bill Tolhurst, VSM, 2000).
Leah A. Zeldes, "Miracle Whip: Boon or blech? Fans and foes mix it
up," Dining Chicago (August 25, 2009).

Chapter 5

Primary sources in this chapter include interviews and correspondence with Chief Scott Folsom, Retired Chief Mike Roberts, Lisa Serio, K9 Officer Jon Richey, and K9 Officer Michael Serio.

Jennifer Emily, "Long Snout of the Law: Bloodhounds' talent on trail
of crime gives authorities edge," *Dallas Morning News* (May 3,
2001).
Aaron Falk, "Hearing begins for man accused of Salt Lake girl's '98
murder," *Salt Lake Tribune* (June 14, 2011, updated June 29,
2011).

Emiley Morgan, "DNA links man to '98 killing of young girl, experts testify," *KSL News* (June 15, 2011).

Emiley Morgan and Randall Jeppesen, "Judge to decide if man will stand trial for murdering 10-year-old girl," *KSL News* (June 14, 2011).

Pat Reavy, "Man Charged with Murdering Anna Palmer Back in Utah," *Deseret News* (July 9, 2010).

Chapter 6

Primary sources in this chapter include interviews and correspondence with Chief Scott Folsom and K9 Officer Michael Serio.

Alameda Police Department, *Golden State Bloodhound Seminar Roster* (April 7–9, 1999).

Federal Bureau of Investigation, *Crime in the U.S.* (FBI Crime Reporting Program, Criminal Justice Information Services Division, 2010).

Henry K. Lee, "Seminar Puts Dogs' Noses to the Test: Dogs Undergo 'Urban' Training in Alameda," *San Francisco Chronicle* (April 8, 1999).

Michael Mehle, "Bloodhound Tracks Girl Across Town into Foothills," *Rocky Mountain News* (May 23, 1993).

Ruben Ortega (Chief of Police), *Agreement for Use of a Bloodhound* (Salt Lake City Corporation, August 1999).

Jeff Schettler, *Red Dog Rising* (Loveland, CO: Alpine Publications, 2009).

Word problem: Let x = the number of people and y = the number of dogs. Set up one equation for heads and one for legs.

$$x + y = 195$$
$$2x + 4y = 570$$

After a little bit of algebra, isolating x in the first equation and substituting it into the second equation, we get:

$$x = 195 - y$$
$$2(195 - y) + 4y = 570$$

Solve for y in the second equation:

$$390 - 2y + 4y = 570$$

$$2y = 180$$
$$y = 90$$

Substitute the value of y into the above:

$$x = 195 - 90$$
$$x = 105$$

The answer: 105 people and 90 dogs are attending the seminar.

Chapter 7

Primary sources in this chapter include interviews and correspondence with Deputy Chief Terry Fritz, Lieutenant Dave Cracroft, Lieutenant Craig Gleason, Sergeant David Wierman, Chief Chris Burbank, Lisa Serio, and K9 Officer Michael Serio.

Salt Lake City Police Department, Watch Command Logs; Lt. Urry, Lt. Whitehead, and Lt. Jensen (September 1999).

Chapter 8

Primary sources in this chapter include interviews and correspondence with Retired Captain Judy Dencker, K9 Officer Jon Richey, and K9 Officer Michael Serio.

Bob Bernick Jr., "These cops speak softly, carry a lip, er, nightstick," *Deseret News* (February 14, 1978).

Amy Donaldson, "Women's Work: Police: Female Officers are Increasingly Common, but Bias Slows Rise Through Ranks," *Deseret News* (May 3, 1992).

Brent Israelsen, "Police Dogs Will Return to Action on S.L. Streets After 12-year Hiatus," *Deseret News* (January 22, 1990).

Mike Johnson, "The Salt Lake City Police K-9 Squad," *Salt Lake Law Enforcement Journal* (December 2004).

Joseph T. Liddell, "S.L. Police to Disband K-9 Corps Feb. 1," *Deseret News* (1978).

Pat Reavy, "Hound has a nose for police work: JJ has remarkable record of sniffing out criminals, missing folk," *Deseret Morning News* (April 15, 2006).

Linda Sillitoe, *Friendly Fire: The ACLU in Utah* (Salt Lake City, UT: Signature Books, 1996).

"The Terrace." Summary and List of Performers. Lagoon History
Project, http://lagoonhistory.com/project/attractions/the-terrace.

Chapter 9

Primary sources in this chapter include interviews and correspondence
with Chief Scott Folsom, Lisa Serio, and K9 Officer Michael Serio.

Charles F. Dinse (Chief of Police), *Agreement for Use of Trained
    Bloodhound* (Salt Lake City Corporation, April 2000).
"Salt Lake City Police Department's Secret Weapon," *KSL News,*
    segment aired on NBC-Affiliate KSL Channel 5 News (February
    2000).
Salt Lake City Police Department, Case Number 1999-206842,
    General Occurrence Hardcopy; Initial Responding Officer Report
    by Jeffrey Kolva, Field Supplemental Report by Michael Serio
    (October 13, 1999).
———, Case Number 1999-220138, Bloodhound Training and Case
    Record; Field Supplemental Report by Officer Michael Serio
    (November 2, 1999).
———, Case Number 1999-239543, Bloodhound Training and Case
    Record; Field Supplemental Report by Officer Michael Serio
    (November 30, 1999).
———, Case Number 2000-868, General Occurrence Hardcopy;
    Initial Responding Officer Report by Jason L. Hathaway, Field
    Supplemental Report by Officer Michael Serio (January 2, 2000).
———, Case Number 2000-1236, Watch Command Log; Lt. Jensen
    (January 2, 2000).
———, Case Number 2000-1236, Bloodhound Training and Case
    Record; Field Supplemental Report by Officer Michael Serio
    (January 4, 2000).
———, Case Number 2000-13809, Watch Command Log; Lt.
    Whitehead (January 22, 2000).
———, Case Number 2000-13809 and 13812, Bloodhound Training
    and Case Record; Field Supplemental Report by Officer Michael
    Serio (January 23, 2000).
———, Case Number 2000-18453, Watch Command Log; Lt.
    Whitehead (January 29, 2000).

————, Case Number 2000-18453, Bloodhound Training and Case Record; Field Supplemental Report by Officer Michael Serio (January 31, 2000).

————, Case Number 2000-21851, Watch Command Log; Lt. Kirk (February 3, 2000).

————, Case Number 2000-21851, Bloodhound Training and Case Record; Field Supplemental Report by Officer Michael Serio (February 5, 2000).

————, Assignment Request and Resume, Officer Michael Serio (February 27, 2000).

"Teenager arrested in theft, car chase," *Deseret News* (January 30, 2000).

Utah Heritage Foundation, "SLC Public Safety Building," www .utahheritagefoundation.com/saving-places/current-projects/ item/54-slc-public-safety-building.

Chapter 10

Primary sources in this chapter include interviews and correspondence with Lieutenant Glenn Smith, Sergeant Brad Marshal, and K9 Officer Michael Serio.

Michael E. Browne, *Schaum's Outline of Theory and Problems of Physics for Engineering and Science,* Schaum's Outline Series (New York: McGraw-Hill Companies, 1999).

Criminal Background Records, Troy D. Fuller, Information Enterprises, Inc. (June 29, 2012).

Salt Lake City Police Department, Case Number 2001-4656, General Occurrence Hardcopy; Field Supplemental Report by Michael Serio, Field Supplemental Report by Jason Miller, Crime Lab Report by Jeffrey Moline (January 9, 2001).

Brad Smith, "K-9 Tracking: The Most Dangerous Job in Law Enforcement," *K-9 Cop Magazine* (January 2010).

Wasatch Front Police K9 Association, www.wfpk9.org.

Chris Watkins, "Remember Fallen K9 Teams," Officer.com (July 19, 2011), www.officer.com/article/10301216/remember-fallen-k9- teams.

Chapter 11

Primary sources in this chapter include interviews and correspondence with K9 Officer Michael Serio.

Alan Abrahamson, "Excellent and Friendly Games Come to a Close," NBC (archived from the original on March 10, 2010).

Charles F. Dinse (Chief of Police), Letter to Officer Michael Serio (November 29, 2000).

Salt Lake City Police Department, Case Number 2001-93272 and 93296, General Occurrence Hardcopy; Initial Responding Officer Report by Bryce Johnson, Field Supplemental Report by Russell Bartlett, Field Supplemental Report by Daniel Delka, Field Supplemental Report by Patti Roberts, Field Supplemental Report by Officer Michael Serio.

———, Case Number 2002-11745, Watch Command Log; Sgt. Isakson (January 20, 2002).

———, Case Number 2000-11745, Bloodhound Training and Case Record; Field Supplemental Report by Officer Michael Serio (January 20, 2002).

———, Case Number 2000-30300, Bloodhound Training and Case Record; Field Supplemental Report by Officer Michael Serio (February 20, 2002).

———, Case Number 2002-34445, Watch Command Log; Lt. Linton (February 25, 2002).

———, Case Number 2000-34445, Bloodhound Training and Case Record; Field Supplemental Report by Officer Michael Serio (February 26, 2002).

ThinkExist.com Quotations, "Aristotle quotes," (ThinkExist.com Quotations, July 1, 2012), http://thinkexist.com/quotes/aristotle.

United States Department of Homeland Security, *Fact Sheet: National Special Security Events* (Office of the Press Secretary, USDHS, December 29, 2006).

Chapter 12

Primary sources in this chapter include interviews and correspondence with Sergeant Kelly Kent, Lisa Serio, and K9 Officer Michael Serio.

Anthony Bruno, "The Kidnapping of Elizabeth Smart" (Crime Library: Criminal Minds and Methods), www.trutv.com/library/crime/criminal_mind/sexual_assault/elizabeth_smart/1_index.html.

"Lead goes 'nowhere' in search for Utah girl," CNN.com (June 8, 2002).

Nancy Dillon, "Elizabeth Smart faces down her kidnapper in court; Brian David Mitchell sentenced to life in prison," *New York Daily News* (May 25, 2011).

Jennifer Dobner, "Utah's Rachael Alert switches to AMBER Alert," *Deseret News* (April 12, 2003).

"The Elizabeth Smart Story," MSNBC, www.livedash.com/transcript/taken_the_elizabeth_smart_story/5304/MSNBC/Sunday_December_12_2010/531786.

FLIR Systems, Inc. Thermal Imaging Infrared Camera specifications, www.flir.com/thermography/americas/us/view/?id=56784.

Emily Friedman and Alex Stone, "Elizabeth Smart Smiles as Jury Finds Kidnapper Guilty, Rejects Insanity Claim," *ABC News* (December 10, 2010).

Sarah Gibbons, "Missing Children 'Die Within an Hour,'" *International Police Review* (September/October 1998).

Graydon Johns and Carole Mikita, "Elizabeth Smart to work for ABC News," *KSL News* (July 7, 2011).

Kirk Johnson, "Verdict is Guilty in Abduction of Elizabeth Smart," *New York Times* (December 10, 2010).

"Lead goes 'nowhere' in search for Utah girl," CNN.com (June 8, 2002).

Dan Metcalf Jr., "Elizabeth Smart testifies of 'indescribable fear,'" ABC 4 News (November 8, 2010).

Pat Reavy, "Kidnappers' camp well-hidden, well-built," *Deseret News* (April 2, 2003).

———, "Ten-year anniversary: 'Everything changed after Elizabeth,' law enforcement says of missing children cases," *Deseret News* (June 4, 2012).

Matt Schwoegler, "Successful Warm-Weather Infrared Inspections" (The Snell Group, 2011).

Tom Smart and Lee Benson, *In Plain Sight: The Startling Truth Behind the Elizabeth Smart Investigation* (Chicago: Chicago Review Press, 2006).

William G. Syrotuck, *Scent and the Scenting Dog* (Mechanicsburg, Pennsylvania: Barkley Productions, 2000).

University of Utah, *Block U Plaque* (October 2006).

John W. Van Cott, *Utah Place Names* (Salt Lake City: University of Utah Press, 1990).

Washington State Office of the Attorney General and US Department of Justice, *Case Management for Missing Children Homicide Investigation* (Criminal Division, Washington State Office of the Attorney General, May 2006).

Chapter 13

Primary sources in this chapter include interviews and correspondence with Chief Chris Burbank and K9 Officer Michael Serio.

Mike Babcock (Director of Public Relations, Shriners Hospitals for Children), Letter to Chief Rick Dinse (July 3, 2001).

Germplasm Resources Information Network for Plants, *Tribulus terrestris L.*, USDA, ARS, National Genetic Resources Program, www.ars-grin.gov/cgi-bin/npgs/html/taxon.pl?100965.

Murray City Park, Murray City homepage, www.murray.utah.gov.

Scholastic, About Norman Bridwell, www.scholastic.com/clifford/normanbridwell.htm.

Chapter 14

Primary sources in this chapter include interviews and correspondence with Lisa Serio, Deputy Chief Terry Fritz, K9 Officer Jon Richey, and K9 Officer Michael Serio.

Salt Lake City Police Department, Case Number 2004-40476, General Offense Hardcopy, Request to Access Public Records; Initial Responding Officer Report by Joseph L. Clark, Initial Responding Officer Report by Cameron S. Platt, Field Supplemental Report by Michael Serio, Field Supplemental Report by Cale B. Lennberg, Field Supplemental Report by Michael Blackburn, Field Supplemental Report by Officer Alton J. Hedenstrom, Sergeant Narrative by Melody A. Gray, and Investigator F/U Report by Thorsten A. Beger (March 9, 2004).

———, Case Number 2004-40476, Watch Command Log; Lt. T. Doubt
(March 8, 2004).

For the Record, Public Safety News from Tribune Staff and Wire
Reports, *Salt Lake Tribune* (August 20, 2004).

Utah Criminal Code, Felony Conviction—Indeterminate Term of
Imprisonment, Title 76, Chapter 3, Section 203, Utah State
Legislature, http://le.utah.gov/~code/TITLE76/htm/76_03_020300
.htm.

Chapter 15

Primary sources in this chapter include interviews and correspondence
with Sergeant Allen Crist, Sergeant David Wierman, Lieutenant Terry
Fritz, Lieutenant Glenn Smith, K9 Officer Jon Richey, and K9 Officer
Michael Serio.

Alex Cabrero, "Dog Catches Public Enemy No. 1," *KSL News*
(November 11, 2004).

Pomera Fronce, "Police ask for dog-vest donors," *Salt Lake Tribune*
(January 4, 2007).

Salt Lake City Police Department, Case Number 2004-200557, General
Occurrence Hardcopy; Field Supplemental Report by David
Wierman, Sergeant Narrative by Jon Richey, Field Supplemental
Report by Michael Serio (November 11, 2004).

———, Case Number 2004-200557, Watch Command Log; Lt. R.
Linton (November 10, 2004).

US Census Bureau, *2010 Census of Population,* Population Estimates
Program (July 1, 2011).

Chapter 16

Primary sources in this chapter include interviews and correspondence
with Chief Chris Burbank, Sergeant Allen Crist, Lieutenant Melody
Gray, Lieutenant Dave Cracroft, Lieutenant Craig Gleason, Sergeant
Kelly Kent, K9 Officer Jon Richey, and K9 Officer Michael Serio.

Dave Askerlund, E-mail to Deputy Chief Scott Atkinson and K9
Sergeant Jon Richey (March 30, 2006).

Craig Gleason, E-mail to Scott Atkinson, Kyle Jones, John Cardona, and Jon Richey (February 1, 2006).

Justin Hill, "Nose for Service: S.L. police officer's bloodhound finds missing boy," *Salt Lake Tribune* (May 26, 2006).

Kyle Jones (Captain, Liberty Division Commander), Letter to Michael Serio (April 4, 2006).

KSL Team Coverage, "Destiny Norton Found Dead, Suspect Arrested" (July 25, 2006).

Pat Reavy, "Deputy has nose for bloodhounds and getting the most out of them," *Deseret News* (June 9, 2009).

Jon Richey, "The Ripple Effect of Original Thought," *Salt Lake Law Enforcement Journal* (December 2008).

Chapter 17

Primary sources in this chapter include interviews and correspondence with Lisa Serio and K9 Officer Michael Serio.

"Bloodhound sniffs out suspect after wild police vehicle chase," *Salt Lake Tribune* (August 26, 2006).

Nate Cralisle, "Bloodhound sniffs out rape suspect in SLC," *Salt Lake Tribune* (October 10, 2006).

Sam Penrod and Marc Giauque, "Suspected Rapist and Scammer Behind Bars," *KSL News* (October 9, 2006).

Salt Lake City Police Department, Case Number 2006-212685, General Occurrence Hardcopy; Initial Responding Officer Report by Moronae Lealaogata, Field Supplemental Report by Michael Serio (November 21, 2006).

———, Case Number 2006-183389, Watch Command Log; Lt. Ross (October 8, 2006).

———, Case Number 2006-212685, Watch Command Log; Lt. Gleason (November 21, 2006).

Taylorsville Police Department, Case Number 2006-21004, General Occurrence Hardcopy; Initial Responding Officer Report by Brett Miller, Sergeant Narrative by Rosie Rivera, Other F/U Report by Mike Ikemiyashiro, Other F/U Report by Christopher Walden, Other F/U Report by Bryan Marshall, Other F/U Report by Joseph Corbett, Other F/U Report by Shannon Bennett, Field

Supplemental Report by Jaren Fowler, Other F/U Report by Scott Miller (August 25, 2006).

Chapter 18

Primary sources in this chapter include interviews and correspondence with Lieutenant Melody Gray, Retired Captain Judy Dencker, Lisa Serio, and K9 Officer Michael Serio.

Nate Carlisle, "Police pup on job despite cancer," *Salt Lake Tribune* (February 24, 2007).

"Despite Cancer, Dog Finds the Bad Guys," *My Fox Utah,* Fox 13 (February 21, 2007).

Joanne Intile, "Canine Melanoma and the Melanoma Vaccine," Vet Specialists of Rochester, http://vetspecialistsofrochester.com/pdf/OncologyArticles/Canine%20melanoma.pdf.

Gene Kennedy, "Police Discover Drugs During Stabbing Investigation," *KSL News* (April 6, 2007).

Keith McCord, "Police Dog Recovering from Cancer," *KSL News* (February 23, 2007).

"Merial Receives Full License Approval for ONCEPT™ Canine Melanoma Vaccine," PR Newswire, *United Business Media* (February 16, 2010).

Karen Ravn, "Canine treatments may shed light on cancer," *Los Angeles Times* (April 9, 2007).

Pat Reavy, "Girl's lemonade stand to benefit heroic dog," *Deseret Morning News* (September 1, 2007).

———, "Salt Lake City police's top dog hit with cancer," *Deseret Morning News* (January 23, 2007).

Salt Lake City Police Department, Case Number 2007-59550, General Occurrence Hardcopy; Initial Responding Officer Report by Peter Ben Johnson, Field Supplemental Report by Michael Serio, Sergeant Narrative by Chris Ward (April 5, 2007).

———, Case Number 2007-59550, Watch Command Log; Lt. Louis (April 5, 2007).

———, Case Number 2007-84954, General Occurrence Hardcopy; Initial Responding Officer Report by Jared Gilbert and Field Supplemental Report by Michael Serio (May 14, 2007).

Michael N. Westley, "Top cop dog ignores illness, still catching crooks for SLC," *Salt Lake Tribune* (February 21, 2007).

Chapter 19

Primary sources in this chapter include interviews and correspondence with Lisa Serio, K9 Officer Jon Richey, Lieutenant Melody Gray, JoAnne Serio, Joe Serio, and K9 Officer Michael Serio.

American Kennel Club, *AKC Meet the Breeds: Bloodhound* (February 29, 1996).

Melody Gray, "Salty Dawgs Remember JJ at B2V," *Salt Lake Law Enforcement Journal* (August 2008).

Pat Reavy, "Pet cemetery fete to laud police dog," *Deseret News* (May 19, 2008).

———, "Police dog first to be buried in special pet cemetery," *Deseret News* (May 15, 2008).

———, "Store employee stabbed, suspect tracked down by K9 bloodhound," *Deseret Morning News* (January 8, 2008).

Salt Lake City Police Department, Case Number CO 2008-2215, General Occurrence Hardcopy; Initial Responding Officer Report by Richard J. Ashby, Other F/U Report by Antonio Valdez, Field Supplemental Report by Nathan W. Clark, Other F/U Report by Rodney Mulder, and Other F/U Report by Kevin Barrett (January 8, 2008).

———, Watch Command Logs; Lt. M. Gray, Lt. Gleason, Lt. A. Healey (2007).

———, Case Number 2008-32071, General Occurrence Hardcopy; Field Supplemental Report by Nickolas Pearce, Field Supplemental Report by Michael Serio (February 18, 2008).

———, Case Number 2008-32071, Watch Command Log; Lt. Gleason (February 17, 2008).

———, Case Number 2002-206442, Watch Command Log; Lt. Fritz (November 12, 2002).

———, Case Number 2002-206442; Bloodhound Deployment Record and Supplemental Field Report by Officer Michael Serio (November 13, 2002).

————, *Police Chief's Officer of the Year: Officer Mike Serio and K9 JJ*, 27th Annual Salt Lake City Police Department Awards Banquet (May 6, 2008).

Michael Serio, E-mail to Police (ALL) (March 10, 2008).

"Suspected Shoplifter Stabs Store Employee," *KSL News* (January 8, 2008), KSL.com.

Nan Walton, *Partners: Everyday Working Dogs Being Heroes Every Day* (Hubble & Hattie, March 2013).

Chapter 20

Primary sources in this chapter include interviews and correspondence with Lisa Serio, K9 Officer Randy Hunnewell, K9 Officer Tyler Lowe, Chief Chris Burbank, Lieutenant Glenn Smith, Deputy Chief Terry Fritz, K9 Officer Jon Richey, Joe Serio, Salt Lake City dispatch officers, and K9 Officer Michael Serio.

"Retired Police Service Dog Gets a Helping 'Paw,'" *South Salt Lake Newsletter* (April 2009).

Jon Richey, "The Ripple Effect of Original Thought," *Salt Lake Law Enforcement Journal* (December 2008).

Michael Serio and Lisa Serio, "My Life with JJ," *Salt Lake Law Enforcement Journal* (August 2008).

Bill Tolhurst, *Police Pocket Training Manual for Bloodhound Handlers*, 1st ed. (National Police Bloodhound Association, 1990), 67.

Epilogue

Primary sources include interviews and correspondence with Sergeant Dave Wierman, Deputy Chief Terry Fritz, and K9 Officer Michael Serio.

Salt Lake City Police Department, Case Number 2011-142291, Watch Command Log; Lt. Johnson and Lt. Cracroft (August 25, 2011).

————, Case Number 2009-23144, Watch Command Log, Lt. Louis (February 7, 2009).

INDEX

ABOUT THE AUTHOR

Adam David Russ is assistant editor of the *Blue Moon Literary & Art Review.* His short stories have appeared in *Paradigm, The Battered Suitcase,* and the collection *All in the Game.* They have garnered awards from *Writer's Digest, The Baltimore Review,* and *New Millennium Writings* and have been performed at Stories on Stage. He lives with his wife and son in Northern California.